Facilitating

Mike Robson
with
Ciarán Beary

Gower

Published by
Gower Publishing Limited
Gower House
Croft Road
Aldershot
Hampshire GU11 3HR
England

Gower
Old Post Road
Brookfield
Vermont 05036
USA

Mike Robson has asserted his right under the Copyright, Designs and Patents Act 1988 to be identified as the author of this work.

British Library Cataloguing in Publication Data

Robson, Mike
  Facilitating
  I. Title   II. Beary, Ciarán
  658.3

ISBN 0–566–07449–4

Library of Congress Cataloging-in-Publication Data

Robson, Mike.
    Facilitating / Mike Robson with Ciarán Beary.
      p.   cm.
    Includes bibliographical references and index.
    ISBN 0–566–07449–4
    1. Communication in management.   2. Work groups.   3. Conflict management.   I. Beary, Ciarán.   II. Title.
    HD30.3.R82   1995
    658.4'6—dc20   94–29910
                                                                CIP

Typeset in Palatino by Raven Typesetters, Chester and printed in Great Britain by Hartnolls Ltd, Bodmin

Contents

Preface

Over the past 15 years or so the word facilitator has entered business vocabulary and has become increasingly important. To date, however there has been no definitive text that covers the subject and there is considerable confusion about the role itself and the situations where facilitators and facilitative styles can be used to good effect. This book attempts to clarify these matters and recognizes the role as fundamental to good management practice in the future.

The styles of management practised by organizations round the world vary, but are seldom based on any clearly thought through strategy for the better utilization of the human resource. Inaccurate assumptions are often made about the skills that people possess, or do not possess, what does and does not motivate them, and the extent of their interest in the process of improving the way that the organization operates. More often than not people assume a minimum ability and willingness, managerial behaviour operates on these assumptions, and management receives what it deserves; which is all a terrible waste of the real talent that exists at all levels of organizations round the world. Even where more positive managerial attitudes exist, a lack of knowledge about how to tap the potential of the human resource for the benefit of the organization itself and the people that work in it often prevails.

Facilitators are agents of change who, depending on their level of skill, and on the way they are deployed, work on helping individuals, groups and the organization as a whole to develop and improve performance. This book is about these issues and how appropriately skilled facilitators and facilitative management styles can help to unlock the unused potential of the organization and the people in it.

Throughout the book, those that the facilitator works with are called customers. This is for two main reasons. First it reflects the very useful idea that all work done in organizations should be seen as being done for a customer, whether internal or external and that this applies to the facilitator role as well as to any other. The second reason is that facilitators will, for the most part, be dealing with 'healthy' individuals and groups. This distinguishes them from therapists and counsellors who would normally talk of their 'clients', and so it seems sensible to reflect that distinction in the terms that we use.

The book is in five parts. The first deals with the facilitator role itself and the need for those involved in this work to understand individual and group behaviour. Because facilitators are change agents the second part covers the management of change among individuals, groups and organizations. The third part provides practical guidance on the skills that are needed for the role to be performed effectively, and the fourth covers the situations in which facilitators can be used successfully and includes case histories covering a wide range of different organizations and subjects. Finally, Part V deals with the subject of facilitative styles of management, which many people believe is the key to success in performing this difficult job.

Mike Robson

PART I
The Facilitator Role

The task of the facilitator is to develop organizations and people; not in theory, but in practice. Though many useful theories that underpin the role exist, success comes from being prepared to try a wide range of interventions, and to continue to use the techniques that work, but always to be able to explain why we choose a certain course of action, and to predict the likely outcomes. It is both an art and a science, but increasingly, as more becomes known about the way people behave, it is a science with definable skills that can be learned and practised by anyone.

Facilitators, in the way the role is used for the most part today, do not have a line relationship with their customers. This will change over time as the use of facilitative styles of management and leadership increase. Chapter 20 deals with this subject. Facilitators work with individuals, groups, and indeed the organization as a whole, helping to improve performance.

In summary, the role is that of an 'on-line' trainer and developer, someone who helps people as they work on improvement activities either individually or in groups. 'Just in time' theories have demonstrated their worth in many manufacturing situations and the idea of facilitation takes this principle and applies it to the effective development of the organization in general and the human resource specifically. However, most people are not particularly good at retaining knowledge for future use, neither are they particularly skilled at taking lessons learned in theory and applying them in practice in a 'real world' situation. It is because of these deficiencies that so much conventional training and development is wasted. People learn most from what they do, and, if this learning can be properly structured, their learning will be that much more effective. So the facilitator works with customers in 'real time' and uses the events that happen here and now as the building blocks of future development activities.

To understand the role of the facilitator, we also need an understanding of some of the main issues that affect the development of groups and individuals. Chapters 3 and 4 cover these subjects.

1 The origins of the facilitator role

The term facilitator first came to prominence with the introduction into the West of Quality Circles in the late 1970s. Quality Circles are a mechanism for encouraging the involvement of the workforce in problem-solving and improvement. Groups of employees working for the same supervisor or first line manager meet voluntarily on a weekly basis to identify, analyse and solve their own work-related problems.

It was soon realized that if such a process was to work, the members and leaders of such groups needed to receive training in elementary problem-solving skills, and that this would best be provided 'in situ' during the course of the weekly meetings. It was not the task of the person providing this training to solve the group's problems but rather to give the leader and the members the wherewithal to do so in an orderly and professional manner. Hence the title facilitator, someone whose task is to make things easy for those working on the problem.

The importance of the role in supporting Quality Circles was quickly appreciated, and it became a standard feature of introducing this particular approach. Unfortunately though, poor or non-existent training in understanding facilitation and developing the necessary skills, contributed to the early demise of Quality Circles in many organizations. As is so often the way, the organizations concerned blamed the approach, claiming that it did not work, rather than recognizing their own ineptitude in introducing and sustaining it. It does work if it is introduced with skill and care, if properly trained facilitators are utilized to support the groups as they work towards self-sufficiency, and if the managerial process continues to be actively and obviously committed to it over time, not as an add on, but as a fundamental part of the way it wants things to be done.

From these relatively humble beginnings the potential of the role in other situations started to be recognized. Today there are examples of chief executives of large international organizations that employ the services of personal facilitators, a trend much to be encouraged given the amount of potential for improvement among most people who occupy such roles. Facilitators in these situations attend the same meetings as the chief executive, and they work together to review performance afterwards, by the facilitators using a process of eliciting self-assessments and also giving their own feedback they work on improvement possibilities. In other organizations, facilitators, in their role as developers of individuals, are deployed at different levels, and in some, people who are particularly knowledgeable and skilful are utilized as full-scale, internal, Organization Development consultants.

Though the original conception of the role was as an 'on-line' trainer, in practice this is, and always has been, a relatively minor part of the true job. The origins of the facilitator role as it is performed now, by those who have been properly trained, are to be found in the work of Kurt Lewin, Carl Rogers and Edgar Schein.

Kurt Lewin was a researcher into the behaviour of groups, and was the person who invented the term 'group dynamics'. Working in the 1940s he realized that most groups did not perform as well as they should have done judging by the capabilities of the individual members, and he set out both to explain this and to provide tools and mechanisms that would help groups diagnose and confront the problem. Lewin recognized that small groups established for whatever purpose tended to be obsessively concerned with the completion of their task, and paid little or no attention to the way that they were going about it. He further realized that virtually all the difficulties faced by such groups were to do with the way they were doing their work, the process. He saw that successful groups were those that actively and consciously managed the process, rather than being entirely 'task-mesmerized'. Although Lewin's work was recognized and valued by fellow researchers, behavioural scientists and Organization Development consultants, it did not permeate organizations in any wholesale way. It is through the role of facilitator that much of his work is given its practical expression today.

The process of group working looks at how the group is doing its work rather than what it is trying to do. It is a combination of a wide variety of factors any of which may be having an important influence on the group at any particular time. For example whether members are really listening to each other will obviously have an important impact, as will the procedure that the group uses to address its problem, the decision-making method used and whether or not a member of the group is dominating proceedings and preventing others from contributing. Understanding and managing the complex dynamics of a group is critical to success, but experience indicates that most people find it difficult, especially at the beginning, to manage the process whilst at the same time working on the task. The facilitator, when working with groups, is responsible for observing the process and pointing out to the group if there are any process issues that are impeding progress.

Carl Rogers developed an approach to counselling and therapy that was 'client-centred'. He recognized that the ownership of the client was vital to the success of any counselling relationship and that a set of skills were needed to develop this in practice. Facilitators, for the most part, are dealing with individuals and groups that are at least relatively 'healthy', unlike Rogers, but there are distinct similarities in some of the attributes that are necessary for success. Because they are developers of people in organizations, facilitators require the sort of skills that Rogers recognized were important in any truly 'client-centred' approach, and they use them routinely in drawing out of the individual or group an analysis of the situation and a preferred way of addressing it.

Edgar Schein, the third core influence on the role of facilitator, introduced the idea of process consultancy as a way of generating high levels of ownership in the client. He distinguished between 'expert' consultancy where the consultant tells the client what the right answer is, 'doctor/patient' consultancy where the consultant diagnoses the illness before providing the cure, and 'process' consultancy where the client is assumed to have the solution, but may not know it or may not know how to access it. Many of the skills of the process consultant are in expert questioning that is successful in eliciting the appropriate self-diagnosis.

The initial expectations that most people seem to have of the consultant role are of an expert who is brought in to tell us the answer to our concern or problem. While this is an appropriate approach in some situations, there are many where it is not, indeed where it is actively counter-productive.

Organizations regularly call in outside consultants to conduct investigations and to recommend solutions to a range of issues. The work is usually done with at least a degree of skill, and yet so often nothing actually happens after the consultants have presented their findings and left. The issue here is an ever-present danger of the ownership leaving with the consultants, and where this happens people in the organization are likely to become frustrated and the consultants are likely to acquire a bad reputation, yet this scenario frequently occurs.

The issues are much the same for the facilitator, who is in many ways an internal consultant, which is why the subject of ownership is so vitally important to anyone who is involved in this role. Right from the early days the effective facilitator has been concerned to help individuals and groups achieve, and those who have been well trained have always known that this involved more than simply saying what should be; indeed that this approach was likely to do more harm than good. It was perhaps inevitable in the early years, given that even many of the people who were running training courses on the subject had no real understanding of it, that many facilitators would be unable to perform the role properly and that they would end up damaging the very process that they were supposedly trying to help. Unfortunately this still happens today.

Having studied the facilitator role over the years, trained many hundreds, if not thousands, of people to practise it well, and observed the damage caused by people who have not been properly equipped, I have concluded that facilitators, if they are to be successful, need to be trained to understand the true origins and purpose of the job, and need to be helped (facilitated) as they begin to practise their newly developed skills.

2 Understanding the facilitator role

In this chapter we begin to look at some of the ingredients of the facilitator role and some of the important issues that we need to bear in mind as we approach the work.

Learning styles

People are different in many ways and one of them is their preferred method of learning. The traditional assumptions that were made about learning gave the responsibility for the process to the teacher or trainer. It is assumed that 'teacher knows best', and that the role of the 'student' is to listen, memorize and be able to repeat. Traditionally it was believed that learning was a process of acquiring and remembering ideas and concepts, primarily in the classroom away from the distractions of everyday life, the job and so on. This is a description that many of the older ones among us will relate to as it describes the whole of our school experience. It is still, remarkably, the model most commonly used; remarkable because of all the possible methods it is the one that works least well!

A more fruitful approach, especially when dealing with adults, which facilitators will be for the most part, is to change the nature of this often unwritten 'contract' to one which places the responsibility on both the trainer and the trainee, the facilitator and the customer. If it is to be successful, we should also recognize that we remember about 10 per cent of what we hear, about 50 per cent of what we see, and about 75 per cent of what we experience, so experiential learning models are preferable wherever it is possible to use them. We need as well to recognize that teaching that is applied to meet individual learning objectives is likely to be more powerful than generalized learning, and ideally we should be able to tailor our approach to the particular way that different individuals prefer to learn.

In this respect Kolb's work on learning styles can be of great use to facilitators. He identified four different ways of learning which are first, by concrete experiences, second by reflective observation, third by abstract conceptualization and fourth by active experimentation. He found that, although any one person's learning style reflects a combination of these four, people have a tendency to prefer one or two methods. From the point of view of the learner there may be an advantage to be gained from expanding the learning styles that are used, and certainly from the facilitator's there is a clear necessity to try to understand and take into account the preferred style of the customer, since this will have a pronounced effect on the results that are achieved.

For example, if as facilitators we work on the assumption that a particular person prefers to learn by abstract conceptualization of the issues when in fact he or she will only be moved by concrete experience, then we will not achieve very much; we will only serve to annoy and frustrate. With this in mind we should be sure to take this issue into consideration when planning our interventions and should have the ability to adapt what we say and how we say it in the light of what is most likely to engage the person or people we are dealing with.

The first learning mode is by concrete experience, which means by being involved; people who learn purely in this way emphasize what they feel rather than what they think. These are people who are concerned with what is happening now, rather than with theories and models, they see the world through their intuition rather than through any systematic or scientific approaches.

Reflective observation is the second mode which implies gaining an understanding of events by careful observation of ideas and events. Purists here would prefer to reflect on what they see rather than to rush in and act, indeed they are more concerned with thinking about things than doing something about them since they are more concerned with understanding than doing. People who use only, or prefer, this learning style tend to be good at seeing the implications of ideas.

In the same way that those who prefer to learn only by concrete experience do so by feeling rather than thinking, those who prefer abstract conceptualization learn by thinking rather than doing. These people are most concerned with having theories and models to which they can subscribe, and being able to apply disciplined and rigorous analysis in the learning situation. They want the learning process to be systematic and capable of quantitative analysis.

The final learning mode is active experimentation. Here the emphasis is on achieving things through an active process of involving people and getting them to take action rather than starting from a need to understand. Active experimenters are the pragmatists of our world, concerned primarily with what works, and much less about abstract concepts such as what is right or true.

Kolb's work tells us that very few people's preferred learning style is a pure version of one of the four described, rather that any individual tends to be an amalgam of the four, but with certain preferences. Drawing on his research, he was able to identify four basic learning styles that cover most people. He called these convergers, divergers, assimilators and accommodators. There is nothing inherently right or wrong about any of these preferred styles; from the facilitator's point of view it is simply a matter of understanding anyone we are dealing with from this point of view so that we can be sufficiently prepared and can therefore adopt the approach that is most likely to succeed.

A 'converger' is someone whose strength lies in problem-solving, decision-making and the practical application of ideas. These people prefer situations where there is one right answer, they prefer technical tasks rather than issues to do with people.

A 'diverger' is imaginative, very aware of, and interested in, underlying values. They tend to be able to see things from different perspectives and are suited to issues that require the generation of ideas. 'Divergers' are interested in people rather than things.

An 'assimilator' is able to pull together different ideas, facts and theories into an integrated whole. They are more interested in developing elegant concepts than in people or the practicability of their ideas.

An 'accommodator' wants to get things done, to become involved in the practicalities of carrying out plans, and to have new experiences. They are happy in uncertain situations where trial and error is the preferred problem-solving process, and where there is a requirement to use information gleaned from outside sources rather than from their own analytical ability.

As facilitators we will be dealing with all sorts of people and certainly we will come across people who reflect all four of these stereotypes. It is clear from the descriptions that different approaches will be needed if we are to be successful with such a wide variety of people. Skilled facilitators are able to work effectively with anyone, not just those that mirror their own particular preferences.

These four preferred learning styles are clearly very different. Without being particularly conscious of it, people are either 'turned on' or 'turned off' by methods of influence that either match or do not match their preferred style. If we think about it carefully we will all be able to recall examples of where we have been successful or not as a result of using the appropriate or inappropriate method. For the vast majority of us the trap we fall into is of assuming that everyone thinks like and learns like we do, and so we plough on and use the methods that would appeal to us, rather than thinking about it from the point of view of our customers. It is a key part of the facilitator's job to be aware of such dangers and to have the knowledge and the skills to avoid them.

The process

The manner in which the facilitator achieves the objective of developing people and helping them to improve their performance is basic to understanding the role since it is different from traditional approaches. We tend to be brought up with the idea that life concerns achievement and that this should be virtually our exclusive aim. This is reinforced at home, at school and most certainly at work. There is nothing intrinsically wrong with this except that it produces what could be described as 'task mesmerization'. In fact, we are here to obtain results, it is just that most people spend at least some of their time preventing themselves from doing this. This happens everywhere and in all walks of life, and is the phenomenon where we become so obsessed with the achievement of the task that we see nothing else, not even the very issues that are preventing us from reaching our goals.

Most people are at least adequately equipped in a technical sense for the job or task that they have to perform. In fact most people are more than competent in this respect. So why is it that when people are working either together or alone so often they underperform, things seem to go wrong, the process feels unsatisfactory?

We have probably all experienced this when working in groups. Someone once said that if you put a number of sane, intelligent people together to work on a problem or issue, the end result is 'collective madness'! The reason for this is that most people have no coherent understanding of the important factors that influence the group as it does its work. In other words they have no understanding of group dynamics or group process as it is now commonly termed. The management of group process is fundamental to success since 95 per cent of the problems that groups face are to do, not with the lack of technical expertise of those involved, but with a lack of understanding of group dynamics and how to manage group process.

It is the facilitator's job, when working with groups to help prevent those involved from falling into these traps. In doing this expert facilitators will utilize the vast reservoir of knowledge and the tools and techniques that have been developed to help people understand the way groups work and how they can improve their performance. This subject is dealt with in more detail in the chapters in this book on Understanding Groups and Changing and Developing Groups.

With individuals the situation is, obviously, different. Behind the facade of confidence that most people display there tend to be many fears and doubts. Thoreau once said 'the mass of men lead lives of quiet desperation'. We have our hopes and our ambitions but we often have little expectation of being able to achieve our goals, still less our dreams.

We are also blocked by the 'comfort zone' within which we operate. This does not mean that we are all comfortable, rather that we become accustomed to a range of experiences, a range of successes, a range of failures and we come to accept them and be comfortable working within those limits. It is just as uncomfortable to succeed 'too much' as it is to fail 'too much' and so we tend to make sure that we gravitate to what we are used to, our 'comfort zone'.

In working with individuals facilitators do not tell the customer what to do. We try to elicit from the people we are working with what is their analysis of their particular situation, and then we help them to build their own plan for their ongoing development, or at least the next steps that they want to take. We also give support and encouragement as this process takes place and help in the planning of further steps.

We should recognize that, since our job involves helping people to develop, which means change for the better, we are involved in the process of helping them to question beliefs that impede or prevent progress being made. Put another way, we are trying to help people to release themselves from the strait-jacket of their present comfort zone and to set themselves more exciting, beneficial and rewarding goals than they otherwise would. We do not set the goals for them, but we can provide a structure that works, and by using our skills we can help people confront and address the necessary issues positively and successfully.

In doing this work the trained facilitator will be using the knowledge and skills that have been developed over the past

20–30 years in client-centred therapy and neuro-linguistic programming. This subject is covered in more detail in Chapter 4 of this book.

So the role of facilitators is concerned with initiating a process which helps those that we are working with to achieve their tasks and goals more effectively than they would otherwise do. Though we are not directly concerned with the task at hand, whether it concerns individuals or groups, we are none the less very interested in our customers actually achieving whatever it is that they are working on, since if they do not there is no point in our being involved.

We work with the process to achieve a fuller and better exploration of the task, whether it is a problem that a group is tackling, or a development issue with an individual. We utilize a process that will ensure that the opportunities presented by the task are more fully explored than they would otherwise be. Having done this we concern ourselves with the achievement of the task, again through ensuring that the process of so doing is sound.

Facilitators are profoundly interested in their customers' achievement of the task, and they understand that their help and influence concentrates on the process which otherwise would not be managed effectively, if at all.

Ownership

Whether working with groups or individuals the facilitator's main aim is the self-sufficiency of the customers, the idea that they carry on with the process of development having the knowledge, skill and motivation to do so. This is an important issue in its own right since, though it may sound obvious, it is actually counter to the way that we are brought up to think and to behave. We tend to be taught to be very individualistic, certainly within Western cultures, and so we look for ways of reinforcing our own contribution and making ourselves the centre of things. We are likely to want to say things like, 'Well, you remember when I told you that you should do that', or 'I guess it was the discussion we had that finally made you decide to do it!'

and so on. This is not lost on the people that we are dealing with, who are likely either to feel that they are in a subservient role, or that they are being manipulated, or that since none of this is their idea anyway that they do not own it and so they do not need to do it unless pressed by the 'initiator', and then probably under duress.

Fundamental to the effective performance of the facilitator role is the notion that we are helping, not doing, and that the ownership of the agreed actions, the actions themselves, and the credit for them lies with our customers not with ourselves. If there is any glory then we only bask in the reflected part of it. If we do more than this it will undermine the effectiveness of what we do.

I was recently working with a board of directors whose managing director was, according to his colleagues, behaving in a way that was demotivating them and causing a range of problems in the organization. Over a period of time we confronted some of the most important of the issues, and did so quite successfully. Then, during one particular meeting, one of the directors suddenly said 'It's really great to have Mike here, he's helped us sort things out in a way that we could never have done by ourselves'. He meant well but I knew that the compliment would be difficult to recover from! Sure enough, for the next few months my dealings with the managing director of that company were dominated by his telling me, in a variety of ways, that it was him and them, rather than me, who had made the improvements. Facilitators do not concern themselves with self-aggrandizement in this traditional and very direct way.

What many people say at this juncture, of course, is that if those that we are dealing with do not directly see the benefits of our work, then they are likely to undervalue it, or even to think that we are doing nothing and so dispense with our services! This is an issue that concerns many facilitators, and quite rightly. The point here is that our customers have bought into a process that will help them to improve, and this is different from buying a person who tells them what to do to improve. Positive marketing of the results of the work that we do is required, but the lesson is that it should be expressed in relation to the process rather than the person.

If the director mentioned earlier had said, 'This process is great, it's helping us to improve the way we're working together', the reaction would have been very different because the ownership would have been retained within the group, and the ego needs of those involved would have been protected.

It is a constant temptation to opt for self-aggrandizement and it will always fail. Talk about the process and the results that are being achieved through it, that is how to 'market' the value of the facilitator role. It is, of course, important that demonstrable results are achieved by those that we are working with, since these are the most eloquent proof of the value of this way of doing things.

Results orientation

Activities concerned with the training and development of the human resource have historically been viewed as 'soft', often ill-defined, rarely measured in terms of effectiveness, nice, but dispensable if other issues to do with 'real work' arise. It has not gone unnoticed that very few people who are sent on training courses ever do anything about them when they return to their work, and this, of course fuels the view described above. Quite right too.

All of the research that has been done on the subject of organizational change and development tells us that the only strategies that really stand the test of time are those that concentrate on improving the performance of the organization. Other programmes and initiatives slide, usually ignominiously, into oblivion after a short time. The waste that this involves is both huge and tragic, and involves more than just money. People in organizations are justifiably sceptical about new initiatives that they see as being a temporary trend, and their level of motivation can easily be affected by what they believe is gimmickry, the only purpose of which they see as being to distract them from their real work.

It is obvious that organizations have a vested interest in ensuring the success of their improvement initiatives, and increasingly it is being recognized that skilled facilitators have a central role in achieving this because quite simply they achieve results through the people that they work with. The role involves developing effective and productive relationships, not just 'nice' ones. Of course we are likely to achieve more in our dealings with our customers if we establish rapport, but a good relationship is only a means to the end of demonstrable improvement in the performance of those that we are working with.

'Just in time'

The facilitator role is a response to the clearly flawed traditional way of training and developing people through conventional training programmes. It has already been said that people are often sent on training courses, which they usually enjoy, but do nothing about when they return to their work. The phrase 'a training holiday' is not unknown! The issue here is that people in general are not very good at retaining knowledge for future use, or at putting lessons learned in theory into practice.

It has also already been mentioned that 'just in time' theories have been put to good use in a wide range of manufacturing environments over the past couple of decades, and that the facilitator role takes this basic idea and applies it to the development of the human resource. It does this by cutting out many steps in the developmental process that historically have been viewed as necessary, but in fact have been counter-productive. People learn most from what they do, and if this learning can be structured, the lessons learned will be that much more powerful and useful. Because of this the facilitator is interested in what actually happens in any given situation, and in helping the customer to learn and profit from the experience.

As facilitators then we are concerned with what is happening here and now, not with theoretical abstractions about what might have been. We take the behaviour that is exhibited and encourage the customer or customers to confront it, to learn from it and to use it as a stepping-stone to improvement. This concentration on the here and now cuts out any need to extrapolate learning, and also does away with most, though not all, of the rationalization that is the single biggest impediment to progress.

If lessons are taught in theory, say in the classroom, there is the easy excuse for inaction that 'I wouldn't have done that in the real world' or 'this isn't a real situation'. By dealing only with what actually happens, in real time, in the real world, we are able to cut through this and help people to learn from and to use their experience effectively. Of course our ability to achieve this is in direct proportion to our ability to see and to understand what is happening, and our skill in encouraging those that we are working with to confront the issues raised, but in general the 'just in time' facilitator approach stands much more chance of success than any of the traditional approaches.

So the facilitator role is a complex one that involves us working with real people, with all their individual quirks and eccentricities, in 'real time'. It is about helping them to improve in their own terms and to confront situations that would otherwise remain blocks to progress. Facilitators gain pleasure and fulfilment through the successes of their customers.

3 Understanding groups

Organizations today have to be able to respond effectively to change and the development of groups and teams is a part of this process. The importance of this issue is being realized more and more, to the extent that some organizations are in danger of overreacting and making the development of effective teams the only dimension of their change process, which it will never be.

This overemphasis on effective teamwork often stems from a misunderstanding of what the Japanese have achieved over the past few decades. It is certainly the case that the Japanese recognize the importance of the issue, and to an extent find it natural, since their culture tends to be more group-based whereas the West is more oriented to the individual. It would be a gross oversimplification, however, to assign all the success that they have achieved to this one component. All this having been said, team working is a necessary ingredient, and is one that requires considerable work in most organizations, since the present level of effectiveness is often so low.

It is rather odd that we recognise deficiencies in both knowledge and skill in many areas, and yet many people assume that we all know how to be effective team members, or at least should do, without any training or development in the subject. Even more strange is that it is often senior managers who are the most likely to take this view, are the most defensive about the subject, and are the worst performers when working together. The explanation of this is probably that most people in Western-based cultures value individuality at the expense of teamwork, and are promoted on the basis of their knowledge and skill as individuals. When they come to work in groups or teams they bring their individual competitiveness into the activity, with predictable results. Unfortunately, though, they do not have the knowledge about groups and group working to be able to see what is happening, or the skills to do anything about it.

We cannot escape the fact that a great deal of work is done in groups and teams. Estimates vary and are, of course, influenced by the nature of particular jobs, but on average managers claim that rather more than 50 per cent of their jobs involve working with more than one other person. When asked how truly effective is that portion of their role there are again large differences, but the average rating comes out at between 30 per cent and 40 per cent. This represents a huge area of potential for change and improvement.

Groups and teams are a fundamental part of the management of any change process. The senior team, the board of directors, are jointly responsible for the way the organization is run; they have to decide how their business will cope with the demands of change that they see all around them. It is of paramount importance that they work effectively in deciding what they will do and then manage the process well.

Further down the organization the structure forms people into groups, one way or another, and the ability of most people to achieve their work goals is dependent in some way on being able to work together well. Finally, many problems and improvement opportunities require group approaches if they are to be tackled successfully.

All of this calls for a much higher level of knowledge and skill, concerning groups and group working, to be in place from the top to the bottom of organizations if the change process is to be managed with any real hope of lasting success. Increasingly the issue of the effectiveness of group and team working is being seen as the subject of a change process in its own right, albeit one that should be viewed as a subset of what is necessary in the organization as a whole.

Our understanding of groups, what happens in them and how we can work to make them more effective has developed rapidly over the last 50 years, until now there are libraries full of books on the subject. The importance of the issue was never more eloquently demonstrated than in the mid-1960s when the President of the United States, John F. Kennedy, faced the 'Bay of Pigs' crisis which so nearly plunged the world into a catastrophe of unthinkable proportions. At that time the Cabinet that Kennedy had formed to work with him was generally recognized as containing the most impressive array of intellectual talent that had ever been drawn together to run their country and yet, through a series of ill-judged decisions that they took together, and to which they were committed, they blundered into the disastrous invasion of the Bay of Pigs.

After the fiasco Kennedy, reflecting on what had happened was quoted as saying: 'How could we have been so stupid?' How indeed could a group of such intelligent, able people have taken such ludicrous actions concerning any subject, let alone one of such profound importance? The answer was that the group fell into a number of traps concerning the way that they were working together. They were not aware of this, of course, but the traps are well known to experts in the field of group working. They had assumed that everyone knows how to work in groups, and that all they had to concentrate on was the task in hand.

More recently Margaret Thatcher, the former Prime Minister of the UK, explained in her memoirs her manner of working with her Cabinet. She said that on any particular issue she would put her own view forcefully and then would ask for other comments and contributions. She also talks in disparaging terms about many of her colleagues being weak and 'wimpish' because of the way they responded in Cabinet discussions. Again, anyone with a knowledge of the way that groups operate, whether they are Cabinets, boards of directors, work teams, parent–teacher associations, or the selection committee for the local sports team, knows that the problem she identified was far more to do with her approach than anything else; the reaction of the other members of the group was entirely predictable, just as predictable as the fact that she blamed them rather than recognizing her own responsibility for the situation.

In both these situations the group was contaminated by different dimensions of what is known as 'groupthink', and if this can happen with groups of that nature and stature, it is very likely that similar phenomena are happening in groups and teams in organizations everywhere, including yours. An important part of any organized change process is to change the way that groups are organized and deployed and to give those involved the requisite knowledge and skills.

Group working has been used throughout history to achieve a variety of objectives. The Greeks, for example, used this method as a way of trying to understand the universe and the way that human beings related to each other. The prevailing belief at that time was that the world behaved according to natural laws that were capable of being discovered and learned, and that people's behaviour was in some way linked to these laws. The two keys to unravelling the mysteries of the universe were to observe nature and to understand oneself. Groups were not understood and used in the way that they are today in achieving this. They were viewed as an efficient way of listening to other experts and holding intellectual debates on the subjects being explored. They were not in the least concerned with any emotional content.

If the Greeks ignored emotional content, many of the early religious groups used groups purely to draw out and utilize this very element, often through a process of either physical or intellectual purging. This was the case, for example, with many of the early Christian and Buddhist monasteries.

As industrial developments shifted the population away from a purely agrarian existence, the guilds and trades began to be developed highlighting the need for cooperation both of people within groups and also between different groups. In a sense, at this point, it began to be realized that the group could, in some cases, be more important than the individuals within it.

Certainly from the time of the Industrial Revolution, as people have been drawn together in more and more close physical proximity, we have become more group-based in our different cultures, with groups being formed to fulfil a whole variety of human needs, from sports clubs to political parties, and a whole host of interest groups.

During the 1940s the idea of group therapy began to be developed in earnest. This was, in part based on the recognition that one therapist could help more than one patient at the same time, and so was more efficient, but it was also founded on the notion that people with a similar problem could help each other in a way that was more effective than other methods. There was an explosion of interest in this subject during the 1940s and 1950s both from the point of view of research, and also the establishing of such groups, which are still in evidence today. The likes of Alcoholics Anonymous and Weight Watchers are international phenomena, and seem to be very successful in helping people address their particular challenge.

A parallel development which is important to understand in the history of groups as they are used to create change was that of Laboratory training. This, in practice, took many forms, but involved a largely experiential approach. The prime mover in this development was Kurt Lewin, who for many is the 'father' of group dynamics. The purpose of Laboratory training was to make people more aware of their interactions with others and to develop new and more effective behaviours by experimenting with and experiencing different possibilities, and by receiving feedback from others in the group.

Such 'growth groups', as they became known, came in many shapes and sizes, such as Encounter groups, Marathon groups, Gestalt groups, and probably the best known, T-groups. These, unfortunately, became something of a fad in the 1960s and 1970s, and though many found them invaluable there were many cases of damage being done to individuals who attended them. Some organizations began to run such activities and to send people to the events whether they wanted to or not, as a part of an organizational initiative. The sessions were sometimes run by people who had insufficient understanding or skill, and who did not have the ability to handle eventualities outside the normal. At the time suicides were reported amongst some people who had found the experience too traumatic to bear. As well as being tragic at a human level, it was also very sad for the growth group movement, because, handled well, it had the ability to produce quite extraordinary results.

Chris Argyris, in studying the effect of such activities, came to the conclusion that they worked best for relatively healthy participants, with quite strong egos, who were willing and able to receive feedback from others, and to use it to change and develop themselves. Despite the ongoing potential of this philosophy of learning, the T-group is today largely discredited as an approach by organizations.

No discussion of the history of groups, and the process of managing change in groups would be complete without mention of the Quality Circles phenomenon. The Japanese, after the Second World War, were put under pressure to introduce mechanisms that would improve the quality of their products. At a national level compulsory education was beginning to influence levels of literacy, and was also having an effect on the aspirations of ordinary working people. Statistical quality control techniques were also being introduced and proving their worth in a wide range of environments.

A suggestion made by Ishikawa at this time was for groups of foremen to establish 'book reading circles', so that they could help each other develop the knowledge that they would need in order to play their part in managing postwar Japan. This idea spread rapidly, but soon the circles began to want more than theoretical study, they wanted to become actively involved, so they began to develop as problem-solving groups. The foremen then began to invite their staff to join in and the first Quality Circles were born.

The approach is based on the principle that it makes sense to encourage the workforce to become involved and to use the strength of their brains as well as that of their arms and legs, otherwise they will quickly become alienated from both the place and the process of work. Furthermore it was recognized that those doing the work are likely to be the ones that know most about it, and have ideas about how it could be improved.

From these beginnings Quality Circles became a worldwide movement during the 1970s and early 1980s. Though handled badly by many organizations who saw it as an easy panacea and did not understand how to nurture and sustain it, it still remains an important element in many change processes, though often under a different name.

The basis of understanding the role of such teams in creating change lies in recognizing the importance of feelings of ownership. Quality Circles are a way of giving ownership to teams of people working with their first line supervisor or manager. Membership is entirely voluntary and the team is free to identify the issues, within their work area, that they wish to address. They are given training in systematic problem-solving and the assistance of a facilitator who helps the group to use the various techniques, and importantly to manage the dynamics of the group as it goes about its work.

The facilitator is not a part of the team, and has no responsibility for the actual task itself, other than to advise if the problem selected is either outside the remit of the group, or is inappropriate in some other way. It would be fair to say that the role of the facilitator 'came of age' in this period, and today much of the work that is done by facilitators involves them in helping various types of group, not just Quality Circles, with their work.

Quality Circles represented the first coherent mechanism to utilize groups as a key part of creating overall organizational change and development, and so deserve their place in history, despite the fact that, through no fault of their own, they enjoy only a mixed 'press' today. As has already been said, whatever they are called, they are still an important element in creating and managing successful change.

Other types of problem-solving groups are also widely used today to help in the process of problem-solving and organization development. Task forces and improvement teams often use the same problem-solving structure as do Quality Circles, and invariably benefit from the involvement of a well-trained and skilled facilitator.

As our knowledge of groups and what influences their performance has increased, it has become more feasible for organizations to structure team-building initiatives. There are many variations on this theme, all of which have their adherents. For some organizations 'outdoor development' holds the key to developing effective teams. Here people are taken away from their place of work into an outdoor environment, and are invited to engage in a series of team tasks, often involving considerable physical exertion, and an element of perceived danger, such as absailing. Having completed, or at least attempted, the task the group discusses its performance, aided by a trained facilitator, and draws learning points from the experience. Because the tasks are different and can be quite stretching, the learning tends to be very vivid and memorable, but it has to be said that the true usefulness of this approach depends on the skill of the facilitator in helping individuals and the team to process the experiences, draw analogies with the normal work situation, and commit to improvement actions after the programme has ended.

Another approach involves the group developing its understanding of the different roles being played by people as the group does its work. This method is often based on the work of Dr Meredith Belbin whose research (described more fully in Chapter 6) indicated that there were a number of quite different roles at play in the work of groups. Furthermore he saw that different people had natural preferences and strengths in some team roles rather than others, and that for a group to perform optimally it required a balance of the different roles to be in evidence. The roles that he identified (Belbin, 1981) are summarized below:

- *Company Worker*   This person tends to be conservative, dutiful and predictable, and has organizing ability, common sense, is hard-working and self-disciplined.
- *Chairman*   This person is calm, self-confident and controlled, and has a capacity for treating and welcoming all potential contributors on their merits and without prejudice. Chairmen have a strong sense of objectives.
- *Shaper*   This person is highly strung, outgoing and dynamic, and possesses drive and a readiness to challenge inertia, ineffectiveness, complacency or self-deception.

- *Plant*   This person is individualistic, serious-minded and unorthodox, and has a lot of imagination, intellect and knowledge.
- *Resource investigator*   This person is extroverted, enthusiastic, curious and communicative and has a capacity for contacting people and exploring anything new. Resource investigators enjoy new challenges.
- *Monitor evaluator*   This person is sober, unemotional and prudent, and displays judgement, discretion and hard-headedness.
- *Team worker*   This person is socially oriented, and tends to be rather mild and sensitive. Team workers have an ability to respond to people and to situations and to promote team spirit.
- *Completer finisher*   This person is painstaking, orderly, conscientious and anxious. Completer finishers are perfectionists who enjoy following things through.

Belbin found that teams made up of the most intellectually capable people available, 'Apollo teams' in his terminology, that we might assume would produce the best result, virtually never came first, and often came last, in his experiments. Shades of Kennedy's Cabinet and the Bay of Pigs!

The point of team building using the Belbin model is to develop an understanding of the benefits of balanced teams, and to help the individuals within the team to understand their preferred team roles. In addition it gives them a language to use in assessing and processing their performance, and since people can work to develop team roles that they do not possess naturally, it can help in the process of identifying what could be done to improve the performance of the particular team in question. Again many organizations have used Belbin's ideas extensively and claim significant benefits from so doing. From the facilitator's point of view a working knowledge of group roles is a necessary part of the knowledge base that is required, and this is dealt with in more detail in Chapter 6.

Understanding the history of the deployment of groups in managing change is an important part of the whole picture that has influenced the development of the facilitator role. In summary, since the 1940s there has been an increasing awareness of the need to differentiate between the task that any group is involved in and how it goes about achieving that task, in other words the process. The term 'group dynamics' was coined to act as a catch all for the myriad factors that influence groups as they go about their work. It is well known today that most groups established both in organizations and outside have the technical knowledge to perform their task, and the fact that they often under-perform is more to do with their lack of understanding of group dynamics or group process than anything else. It is one of the most useful roles of the facilitator to assist groups with just this knowledge, and also to help people develop the skills to be able to manage the dynamics of the groups that they are involved in.

4 Understanding individuals

As facilitators, whether we like it or not, we are placed in a role where we have to deal with individuals in their entirety. This is the case whether we are dealing with people purely as individuals, or whether we are working with them in the context of a group, since, obviously, it is largely individual behaviour that constitutes what happens in a group. We usually have no conventional line authority that would enable us as a last resort to say, 'just do it!' and to answer the question 'why?' with 'because I say so'. Because of this, and also because, as a generalization, we know that this approach is not very successful in achieving any self-motivated improvement, we have to try at least to understand what it is that explains the way people act, and to adapt our approach accordingly. This is made rather more complex by the fact that we are dealing with situations where the intervention of a third party is necessary to achieve progress, and that it is often individual quirks that have impeded progress in the past.

If we can accept the assumption that anything we say in relation to individuals is going to be a generalization, and that there will, therefore, be exceptions, there are a number of very useful

31

pieces of knowledge that can help us and can guide our behaviour to make it more effective than it might otherwise be.

Facilitators must start from the current attainment level of the person we are dealing with, a notion that is dealt with more fully in Chapter 8. Then there are a number of useful inputs that can help us to diagnose and to understand at least in a general sense the frame of reference of our customer. The context for this is that we are trying to help the individuals that we are dealing with to create change that will benefit themselves and the organization in which they are working.

Change, if it is to be facilitated rather than simply imposed, requires us to try to understand those that we are dealing with in a number of respects. Important among these are our customers' frames of reference or 'life positions', what motivates them, how the amount of effort they are prepared to expend is influenced by the combination of their desires and expectations, how they handle their feelings in a general sense, and finally what 'language' do they think in.

Based on Eric Berne's work on transactional analysis, Thomas Harris developed a way of helping us to understand individuals in terms of the extent that they see themselves and others as 'OK' or 'Not OK'. This is a well-known, though not so well understood, model that can be of great help when applied with skill and care. Harris put forward the view, which is now widely accepted, that early in childhood people adopt a basic 'life position' which is rarely changed, unless it is worked on consciously, since people tend to reinforce it by a process of selective perception about their experiences in life. Harris's model has the advantage of being simple to understand and of being expressed in non-technical language.

The model describes four 'life positions' that are combinations of whether a person perceives him or herself as 'OK' or 'Not OK', and whether he or she perceives others as 'OK' or 'Not OK':

- *I'm not OK, you're OK* People in this 'life position' tend to see themselves as inferior to others in terms of their competence and ability to influence others. They are lacking in confidence and tend to be beaten before they start. They see others as having all the advantages in life, and express the view that 'it's all right for them . . .'. For people in this position the grass is always greener on the other side of the hill.

- *I'm not OK, you're not OK*   This is a very dangerous 'life position'. People that occupy it tend to see both themselves and everyone else as worthless. They are likely to be paranoid, always concerning themselves with 'conspiracy theories' about what others are doing that might harm them, and so they alienate themselves from both other people and the environment. Such people are often angry and aggressive, but are not prepared to do anything that might improve the situation because they do not see anything as being worth while. In its extreme form this life state can lead to suicide.

- *I'm OK, you're not OK*   People who occupy this 'life position' believe that they can only rely on and trust themselves. They see others as weak and worthless and the cause of anything and everything that goes wrong; they certainly are never to blame in their eyes. Arrogant and insensitive, such people do what they want regardless of the effect it may have on others and, if confronted, are likely to say that if others do not like it then they should leave them alone. Criminals often have this mental set.

- *I'm OK, you're OK*   The final 'life position' involves accepting oneself as being interdependent with other people and the environment. Being 'OK' is not seen in a competitive light, indeed people in this position both see 'OK-ness' in others and want to recognize it and value it as being a part of the business of interdependency.

Both Berne and Harris believed that in early childhood people's experiences led them naturally into one of the first three positions, and that this would shape the whole of their lives unless they actively and consciously worked on making the move in both perception and behaviour to the fourth, 'I'm OK, you're OK', state.

Many people, seeing the rather obvious point, claim to be examples of this fourth 'life position', but for the most part this tends to be an illustration of people's desire to be examples of 'the right answer'. Berne and Harris recognized that such claims were in fact far from the real situation. They saw the 'normal' state being 'I'm not OK, You're OK', and explained this in terms of an infant being entirely dependent on its parents for feeling OK, through feeding, attention, recognition and so on. When the child's immediate needs are not gratified there is a feeling of 'not OK-ness' that the child is unable to do anything about. In this way the child is 'programmed', and the effect will continue until and unless an alternative 'programme' is put in place. Remember Thoreau's observation about 'lives of quiet desperation'.

The other two 'life positions' can be explained as variations on this theme. If young children receive a considerable amount of negative experience from and of the adult world they conclude that both they and others are 'not OK'. Finally there are those who suffer negative experiences but develop an ability to gratify their own needs for positive strokes and therefore come to the feeling that while they are 'OK', the rest of the world is not.

This is a very useful 'shorthand' way for facilitators to begin the process of trying to understand the people they are dealing with, and is important since, clearly, an approach that is based on the assumption that someone is in the 'I'm not OK, you're OK' 'life position', is unlikely to work very well if in fact the actual position is 'I'm OK, you're not OK'.

As facilitators we are in the business of helping people to achieve practical improvements in their performance, rather than in their psychological state *per se*. However, there is little doubt that the most effective people are those who are healthy in a psychological sense, and so it is hard to avoid having an interest in this dimension. We must, though, avoid the temptation to play the 'psychologist game', which is something that most of us are not trained for and anyway is not the purpose of our role. If such changes in the psychological state of those who we are working with do come about, it will be because the practical successes they achieve while working with us cause them to re-evaluate their position and develop this aspect of themselves. It will not be because we have subjected our customers to a programme of amateur therapy, which is a dangerous and self-indulgent course that will do the facilitator's credibility no good at all.

The second subject area that will help facilitators to understand things from the standpoint of their customers is motivation. What motivates people will, obviously, influence both what they want and are prepared to do and will influence how people look at and evaluate the options they are presented with. Perhaps the best known theory of human motivation was the one developed by Abraham Maslow some 40 years ago. It is still of great use to practising facilitators today, not only because it contains much that describes the way people act, but also because it is simple to describe and to understand. It is also a theory that many have come across on training courses that they have attended, so for many it is familiar, albeit that very few people ever use it actively. Facilitators, however, can utilize Maslow's work in a very practical way in understanding the likely motivations of their customers.

Maslow suggests that it is only unsatisfied needs that motivate. An unsatisfied need creates tension, which can be either pleasant or unpleasant, and this creates the energy required to fulfil the need. Once this is done the tension is no longer there, so a satisfied need no longer motivates. Whereas this can be applied to particular individual needs at any point of time, for example if I am hungry I will find something to eat, whereas if I am not I will not, Maslow also saw that he could understand human behaviour more clearly by looking at a number of general categories of need. He established that, at any point in time, a person's unsatisfied needs tended to fall into one particular category, that the person's behaviour would be dominated by trying to meet these needs, and that 'higher level' needs are not even perceived until 'lower level' ones are more or less satisfied. He suggested that there were five such 'bands' which he expressed in a hierarchy as follows:

- *Basic needs* These are the set of needs that must be fulfilled for survival and include air, water, food and so on.
- *Safety* These are the needs to be sure that we are not threatened. In a primitive society this would cover the need for

protection from dangerous predators, but in the developed world job security, for example, would come in this category.

- *Social*   These are the needs for a feeling of belonging and for being accepted in a social sense by others.
- *Ego*   This set of needs is concerned with being viewed positively by others in terms of effectiveness and competence, feeling that we are valued and so developing a sufficient level of self-esteem.
- *Self-actualization*   These are the set of needs concerned with personal growth and challenge. Self-actualization concerns maximizing the use of our potential in every way, regardless of what anyone else might think, and optimizing our performance in our own terms rather than being influenced in our behaviour by the need for the approbation of others.

There are a number of very useful and usable elements of Maslow's theory. In realizing that only unsatisfied needs motivate, and that at any time an individual's unsatisfied needs tend to cluster into one or other of the categories in the hierarchy, he gives us a clue to how we can motivate people to accept the challenge of improvement. His research indicated that very few people's behaviour was dominated by unsatisfied needs in the self-actualization category, in fact through a combination of interviewing and observing contemporary people and also reviewing public and historical figures, he developed a list of fewer than 50 possibilities. It is not a prerequisite to be a famous figure, those self-actualizing people that he found at the time of his research were often private individuals.

In Western society at least, basic and security needs are more or less catered for, apart from the situation where someone may have lost their job and be unable to find another one. This can sometimes, ultimately, cause this category of needs to become unsatisfied and to dominate the behaviour of the person concerned. From the point of view of the facilitator working in an ongoing business, however, this situation is not one that is likely to need handling.

So, if very few people are significantly self-actualizing and the basic and security needs are more or less fulfilled, at least to the extent that they are not predominant, we can conclude that most people we will be dealing with will have their unsatisfied needs clustered in either the 'social' or the 'ego' categories. Facilitators who wish to help those that they are dealing with to be motivated to engage themselves actively in the process of improvement will do well, therefore, to diagnose which of these two levels in the hierarchy of needs is most applicable to the particular person concerned. Given this, any necessary encouragement and advice can be couched in suitable terms. For example if someone seemed to be driven by the need for social integration and acceptance, we could say 'becoming involved will give you the opportunity to belong to a problem-solving group and to work with others on solving an important problem'. If, on the other hand, the individual seemed to be concerned about 'ego' needs, we could say 'becoming involved will give you the opportunity to show what you can do and to make your mark in the organization'.

According to Maslow's theory once the unsatisfied needs at one level of the hierarchy are more or less fulfilled, the next level of unsatisfied needs begin to reveal themselves and become those that the individual will concentrate on meeting. This process however, is not just a one-way progression. To pick up the point noted earlier, someone could at a certain point be concerned at fulfilling ego needs. This same person could, say, be made redundant and could find it hard to obtain another job. Over a period of time in this case it is possible, even likely, that the dominant category of unsatisfied needs could 'regress' first to social, maybe expressed as the desire to have the family around to the exclusion of others, and then, maybe, to security issues if the threat seemed great enough. There is no right and wrong in any of this, what we have here is a description that can help us to understand those that we are dealing with from the point of view of what is most likely to help galvanize them into action, which is one of our roles as facilitators.

The third important subject that facilitators need to understand and use when dealing with individuals concerns the interaction between desire for a particular outcome and their expectation that it is achievable. Victor Vroom researched this area and found that the effort that people were prepared to put into achieving an outcome was equal to their desire for it multiplied by their expectation that the effort would achieve the required result. All facilitators need to understand this formula especially the effect of the multiplication sign. I have a very high desire to win the football pools, yet I do not do them! How can such irrational behaviour be accounted for? The point is, of course, that I have a zero expectation that the effort would be worth while. A million units of desire multiplied by zero equals zero.

This is important to the facilitator in two respects. First we need to be aware that when we are dealing with individuals and their motivation we are dealing not with two separate issues in desire and expectation, but with both at the same time in a complex intertwined relationship. The second important issue stems from experience in having worked with many people and many organizations over the years. Organizations, usually in the shape of the management process, are almost invariably inclined to judge an unwillingness amongst members of staff to become involved as indicating a lack of desire. These same people, however, again so often explain their reasoning in terms of a lack of expectation that it will prove worth while, not just in their pockets, but in terms of the use of their energies. People in many different organizations so often say things like, 'if it weren't for . . . (the management) . . . we could really get this place sorted out, which would be great' that it cannot possibly be either a coincidence or a conspiracy.

The message for facilitators is clear; we should be very wary of accepting an apparent lack of desire on the part of the individuals that we are dealing with. It will be better to use the working assumption that what is in evidence is probably a lack of expectation, often born out of bitter experience. We should try to understand why this is and to raise their level of expectation, at least a little. People are unlikely to develop high levels of expectation simply because we say it is a good idea, and to be honest we do not require this in the first instance. To go back to the football pools example, a million units of desire multiplied by say one unit of expectation would be enough to encourage me to do something. From our point of view as facilitators we are initially concerned to encourage people to become involved, not necessarily with missionary zeal from the outset. The success that will come out of the process itself will achieve this if anything will.

The next issue that facilitators will do well to bear in mind as they are working with and trying to understand individuals, concerns how people handle their feelings. Working in organizations can be a very frustrating experience, and it certainly evokes strong emotions in many people, that they then have to deal with. Karl Albrecht developed a useful model which describes the different ways that people go about doing this, and offers some clues for facilitators in dealing with some of the reactions they are likely to come across.

Albrecht identified three different ways that people come to terms with their strongly felt emotions, the first of which he called 'suppression'. This involves the person in using a range of devices aimed at denying the existence of the strong emotions, avoidance of any mention or thought of them, emotional or physical withdrawal and rationalization. The effects of this are that the person concerned tends to become very rigid in dealings with others, detached, unable and unwilling to form close relationships with others from that environment.

The second mechanism that is adopted by some involves 'capitulation' to the feelings. In this state people will tend to blame others, make instant judgements, overreact and become pre-occupied with the situation that gave rise to the feelings in the first place. The likely consequences of this reaction include a general feeling of helplessness and dependency, low self-esteem, an inability to maintain an attitude to life that is in any sort of balance, and a lack of interest in planning for the future.

These two sets of responses are clearly unhealthy whereas the third, 'accommodation', involves a recognition and acceptance of the strong feelings and the need to work with them actively and to recreate equilibrium. In this state the person's reaction to the emotional state is more balanced and appropriate, and since self-esteem is high other people can be utilized in helping with the coping process. Little time is spent on recrimination and it is possible still to use feelings to handle the situation rather than to deny their existence.

From the facilitator's point of view it is certainly useful to have available a way of interpreting different types of emotional reaction. The model also gives some pointers to what is needed to help people who are either suppressing or capitulating to their emotions. This will involve trying to get people to recognize and accept their reaction, not to blame either themselves or others for it, and to concentrate on maintaining or rebuilding their self-esteem through actively and positively confronting the challenge that is presented by the event that caused the feelings in the first place. In organizations is likely to be any of the many difficult or apparently absurd decisions that are taken and then implemented without thorough explanation to those affected.

Not only are our jobs important to us but also most of us carry a high level of concern and interest for the welfare of our organization, we interpret situations through our own, albeit limited, perceptions, and are likely to have both intellectual and emotional reactions to such decisions especially when they affect ourselves directly, or those around us. Because of this facilitators need to be able to handle negative or unhelpful emotional reactions in a way that transforms them into something more positive, or at least does not stop or impede the development and improvement process.

Finally in this section, it will be very useful for facilitators if they can gain an insight into the way individuals perceive and encode the reality that is around them. Three people went for a walk in the country. They strolled along, side by side. One saw the clouds scuttling across the sky, the way the corn was shaped into patterns by the wind and the many different colours of green and gold and brown. The second heard the rustling of the wind in the trees and the sounds of the birds, while the third touched the bark of the trees, felt the wind on her face, and was moved by the beauty of nature. After having been on exactly the same walk they compared notes, and of course found that they had experienced profoundly different things.

This is important for facilitators in understanding the people that they are dealing with. We see, think about and express our version of reality in very different ways, but fortunately for the observant, there are clues that can help us to understand the different codes. These clues are first in the words that we use and second in the movement of our eyes.

We all experience the world through our five senses; sight, hearing, feeling, smell and taste. We do not use all these senses in the same way and to the same degree, rather we represent our individual world by using them to a greater or lesser degree. The three people on the walk mentioned above are a case in point. One was primarily a visual person, the second was auditory and the third was most concerned with feelings.

If we had asked them to relate their own experience, the first would have said something like; 'Did you see that! It was brilliant. The sun streaming down, fabulous colours, I've never seen anything like it, it was a picture.' We can see here that the words being used are visual, 'see', 'brilliant', 'seen', 'picture'.

The second person would have said something like, 'I love being in tune with nature. The sound of the wind, the song of the birds, did you hear those skylarks? It was so loud yet everything was in harmony.' Here the way of representing the experience is mainly auditory, 'in tune', 'sound', 'song', 'hear', 'loud', 'in harmony'.

Finally the third person would have said something like, 'I've never felt so closely in touch with nature. It sent a shiver down my spine as the wind brushed my face. The smooth feel of the grass and the roughness of the bark of the trees put me in contact with reality.' This person represents the world primarily through feelings using words like, 'felt', 'shiver', 'brushed', 'feel', 'roughness', 'in contact'.

The importance of this for the facilitator is that understanding the 'representational system' of the people we are dealing with gives us a valuable clue about the way that they think. This, in its turn, tells us the 'code' that they are most likely to respond to in our dealings with them. The three main systems that people use are visual, auditory and kinesthetic (feelings) and everyone has a particular pattern that they use routinely and without being conscious of it. Whereas we all use all three systems at one time or another we also have biases towards one or other way of thinking, and this has an important effect on our interactions with others.

Strangely enough, eye movements tell the same story. If some-one's eyes go up, either to the right or the left, it indicates that they are visualizing. If the eyes go up and to the right as we are looking at the person, he or she is remembering something as a picture. If they go up and to the left a picture is being con-structed.

If the eyes move laterally it indicates that the person is in audi-tory mode. To the right means that sounds are being remem-bered and to the left means that they are being constructed.

If the eyes move down and to the right it indicates that the per-son is having an internal dialogue, talking to themselves if you like, and if they move down and to the left it tells us that they are experiencing feelings.

These movements apply to normally organized, right-handed people – for left-handers they are reversed. So, with this informa-tion we are able to understand the way that the person we are dealing with thinks and with this information we should be able to respond using the same 'code' and thereby both build empa-thy and also make it easier for the person to relate to our contri-butions.

In this chapter we have explored some of the important dimensions that will help us to understand the individuals that we are dealing with. Of course, the issues covered only represent a fraction of the elements that make us the unique beings that we are, but none the less they will prove very useful for the practis-ing facilitator as a backdrop against which the practical work of helping people to improve their performance can go on. We need to use information such as this to help and guide us in our work whilst at the same time recognizing that we do not understand our customers fully. Because of this, we require sensitivity to the myriad other dimensions that may be having an effect, and we certainly must not be rigid or inflexible in our approach. The aim for the facilitator should be that the information presented here becomes a normal part of the way we approach our role and that we feel comfortable enough with it to use it flexibly.

PART II
Managing Change

The management of change among organizations, groups and individuals is perhaps the biggest challenge that faces organizations today, and the facilitator role is concerned with helping to confront it successfully.

In 1970, Alvin Toffler in his book Future Shock, said `change is now the only constant'. He has been proved right in a way that might even have surprised him. Change is all around us, and is occurring at an exponential rate that is almost frightening. Unless managements are able to cope with the demands imposed by the changes that they face, their organizations are unlikely to survive. No one has any automatic right to survive and succeed. Look at the comparative fortunes of IBM and Microsoft, but also realize that if, by the time of publication of this book, circumstances have changed, it will only serve to re-inforce the point. As Bob Dylan once said:

`The slow one now
Will later be fast . . .

And the first one now
Will later be last
For the times they are a-changin'.
(Bob Dylan, *Writings and Drawings*, Panther, 1972)

Without over-dramatizing the issue, the evidence around us indicates that organizations need to develop the ability to manage change in a coherent way if they are to remain in business. Unfortunately many managers currently do not have either the knowledge or the experience to manage change successfully, and most organizations treat the management of change in a purely ad hoc and unsystematic way, but then rationalize their behaviour after the event when things go wrong.

Underlying any coherent organizational change process are the assumptions made about people and the skills used in educating, training, developing and involving the managers and other employees of the organization in the change process itself and the ongoing job of running the organization thereafter, which of course involves dealing with yet more change. Increasingly it is argued by managers that people are the most important resource available to organizations and that successful change will only be achieved if people accept their part and have appropriate and skilled leadership to guide them through it. Considerable evidence supports this view, but it is contaminated, to an extent, by the experience of those who propound it, but either are paying lip-service or do not have the necessary knowledge, skills or experience to manage it successfully. Because of this there are still those who support traditional views and there are certainly still many managers who do their job on the basis of traditional assumptions even though some of them do not realize it.

Facilitation as a skill and a science is very much a product of the modern school, but we must see it in context if we are to be able to understand it properly. Facilitators, fundamentally, are concerned with helping to create effective change and development, whether at the level of the individual, the team or the whole organization, and so we need to consider each of these contexts in turn.

5 Changing and developing organizations

Ever since organizations have existed attempts have been made to develop and change them. Certainly over the past hundred or so years this process has become more intense, and today it could be seen as an ongoing requirement for any organization that wishes to survive and succeed. There is no need in this book to explain in intricate detail all the different contributions that have been made over the past one hundred years in the field of organization change and development, but it is useful for us to understand the current trends that make the role of the facilitator fundamental to making progress. Probably the most powerful trend is that of change, and the need to handle it sensitively and proactively. The breadth of knowledge and skill that expert facilitators bring to bear is of significant value in what otherwise can seem a chaotic and unmanageable state of affairs.

Enough has been said and written about the whole subject for us to accept that the attitudes and behaviour of the people in the organization are very important to the long-term effectiveness of any process of change, development and improvement. Kurt Vonnegut (*The Player Piano*) once said, 'if it weren't for the people, always getting tangled up in the machinery, life would be an engineer's paradise'. Maybe it would, but the people are there, and have to be handled effectively if progress is to be made and sustained.

The issue of people at all levels of the organization, and of their reactions, has always been significant and remains so today. Any facilitator who aims to work successfully with the organization as a whole will require an understanding of the likely reactions and responses of the people within it, and also the different pressures that are brought to bear on people at different levels that affect their behaviour.

In the early part of this century Frederick Taylor developed his famous theory of 'scientific management'. Many of the entrepreneurs who were in business at the time took serious exception to his views on the basis that he was questioning their superior ability, intellect and judgement, and that since they had been so successful for so long, there was nothing significant that he could teach them. Taylor anticipated this negative response from management (some things don't change!), but he was surprised at the response of many workers who resisted his approach on two counts; first because most of the benefits which were gained from their working harder went to the company, and second, many found the idea of being treated like machines extremely objectionable.

Since then there have been many other offerings to tempt those who were keen to improve performance. Human Relations Theory, Motivation Theory, Systems Theory, Organization Development, Job Enrichment, Quality Circles, Total Quality, Business Process Re-engineering, to name but a few; and the core issues remain the same as far as the response of many of the people in the organization is concerned. Many managers either feel threatened by the prospect of a change in the 'rules of the game' which were the very rules that led to their own personal success, or they take the view that since they have achieved success and that they are intelligent and work hard, that there cannot be a better way of doing things. If there were, surely they would have worked it out for themselves and be doing it already.

From the point of view of the workforce the most important

issue remains one of trust, and often revolves round questions of what it is that 'management' is trying to manipulate them into, and even if there is none of this, whether the organization is serious and will retain its expressed commitment, and ultimately whether these particular managers are capable of managing such radical changes in the whole philosophy of work. Trade unions have often been accused of fuelling such fears and sometimes they have, often from genuine doubt, at other times from a fear of losing their own influence, political agendas, lack of understanding – a whole range of possible reasons. Ultimately, however, it is the reaction of the workforce in the organization that is the main concern, and unless they are prepared to commit themselves, and sustain that commitment, no process of improvement will stand the test of time.

Facilitators working with the organization as a whole need to be able to relate to, and to deal with, the prevailing issues at all levels. The skills that they will need are those that are described elsewhere in this book, facilitators also need to understand the main organizational dynamics that cause the situations they are likely to encounter among different levels of management and the rest of the workforce. In practice it is useful to distinguish between the issues as they affect senior management, other managers and the workforce in general, and to highlight how a skilled facilitator can positively influence them.

Senior management is responsible for setting the goals and direction of the organization, and this involves the making of strategic decisions such as the nature and style of improvement activities. We must improve, even to stand still, if we accept the truism that we live in a world where 'change is the only constant', yet not all senior people seem willing to accept this truth in their particular situation. Some do have the vision whilst others are remarkably reactionary.

Those that are reactionary will be defensive about change, believing that the strategies that helped them to the top are the ones that will preserve their own position and that of the organization. They are wrong, but unfortunately it is usually difficult to shift them from this position until it is too late. Internal facilitators will not normally encounter this situation in its extreme form since it is unlikely that they would have a role in such circumstances, but it is not so unusual for external consultants. Where it is encountered the best approach, using the range of skills described in this book, is to gain unequivocal agreement to the fact of change, specifically in the environment concerned, and then to make the point that the great leaders are those that have the vision and also the courage to confront this challenge. The improvement process proposed should concentrate directly on the potential for making the performance of the organization even better than it is at the moment, and the point should be made forcefully that no such process can be accomplished without the understanding and active support of the top. It will not always work, but it is the approach that is most likely to succeed.

Most internal facilitators, however, will be operating in an environment where a commitment has been made, and a process has been started. Many will then see, or at least believe they are seeing, a wavering in enthusiasm and commitment after a period of time. Facilitators fulfil an important role in such circumstances, but they need to understand the three main possible reasons for the situation having arisen.

First, though the senior managers are at the top of the particular organization, in one form or another they are often subject to intense pressure from outside, for example from a parent company or the stock market. Such pressure is very often to improve short-term results at all costs. Though in many ways absurd, it is an intense pressure. It is significant that in Japan, for example, businesses take a much longer-term view. The 'short termism' that is characteristic of so many Western companies leads directly to the 'flavour of the month' mentality that affects so many Western cultures.

In such circumstances facilitators can help to steady the nerves and can assist in constructing the persuasive argument for continuing with the process that has been started. They should also be able to suggest ideas for improvement activities that will yield short-term and visible benefits, and so take the pressure off the demands for immediate results.

The second possibility is that the top management becomes

impatient for results, is seduced by a new theory that is being promoted in business circles, and wants to stop the current initiative and 'really' commit to this new venture as the way ahead. If this happens the predictions of the majority of the people in the organisation about gimmicks is confirmed, and the difficulty of making the next innovation anything but the next in a long line of fads is increased. Generally speaking, senior managers are not stupid, but sometimes they behave as if they are, often because they are imaginative and impatient. In these situations they are prone unwittingly to 'throwing the baby out with the bathwater'.

The facilitator role in this situation is significant. The top manager has had the imagination and courage to commit to change and improvement, but is now in severe danger of negating the effort. First we need an explicit statement about what outcomes are required of the existing process and over what period of time. We may wish to discuss the feasibility of the goals, for example we may want to transform people's attitudes overnight, but it is not necessarily a reasonable and viable objective, and so we would be unwise to judge a process against this criterion. Having gained such a clear statement we should work with the top manager in assessing progress and making plans to increase the pace if this is needed. Secondly we should reinforce the danger of short-term fads, and should position the new initiative that the top manager is interested in, assuming that it makes sense, as a new element within the existing overall process, so that it can be introduced as a natural development rather than as something new and different.

The third reason why the feeling that commitment is waning might arise is because top management do sometimes fall into the trap of thinking that their job is done having set the organization on the road. In fact, to achieve real success, those at the top need to role model the process in everything they say and everything they do, all day, every day, now and for ever. If they don't, why on earth should anyone else?

Again the facilitator can be instrumental in addressing this issue, and the concentration in this situation should be on the issue of leadership. There are many examples, both from history and from contemporary affairs, of the immense power and importance of setting the appropriate example. There are just as many illustrations of the damage that is caused by not doing so, and both can be used to good effect. People in organizations tend to follow the attitudinal and behavioural example of those at the top, it is as simple as that; we tend to get what we deserve when it comes to the behaviour of our employees.

As far as other managers are concerned the issues that the facilitator will have to deal with are rather different. Many middle and junior managers who are performing traditional roles both feel, and are, threatened. Most organizations are massively over-managed if that management is performed in the traditional 'controlling and policing' style. It is, therefore, not surprising that many people in such roles tend to be defensive about initiatives that are designed, in part, to liberate the potential of the workforce, and to empower them to play their vital part in the improvement process.

Successful management encourages the best out of people, and this can only be achieved through facilitative styles of leadership; Chapter 20 deals with this issue. The role of facilitators here lies in helping managers to become facilitators of their own people, not just for an hour a week, but routinely, in everything that they do. The mechanisms for achieving this are dealt with elsewhere in this book, and we need to address the challenge since this is a main feature of organizations today.

In an ideal world we would be able to transform the management process and the day-to-day behaviour of managers overnight, and there would be little need for our services, but of course the world is not ideal, so facilitators also have a role to play with the workforce in general. Because we are working alongside and in parallel with line management we must be very careful not to undermine those who perform these jobs. Equally we should remember that we are concerned with change and development, with improvement from the *status quo*, and this involves the perceptions of the workforce at large.

It is unfortunate, but true, that few organizations have managed to harness the hearts and minds and the full capability of their workforce and to sustain it over time. One of the main reasons for this is that the way that the management role has been positioned and performed has sometimes tended to promote a somewhat adversarial relationship. This may be an uncomfortable and unpalatable notion for many managers, but if you ask the staff it is confirmed time and time again. There are two common causes of this, first that the management process really does evoke this response and, second, that the workforce assumes or perceives that this is the case, even though it is not, and rationalizes events to fit with their preconception.

In both of these circumstances the facilitator can help. The situation where the management process itself is faulty has already been dealt with; facilitators have a role to play in the development of more effective managers. Where the perceptions of the workforce are the issue, facilitators can help, partly by virtue of their being outside the normal chain of command, and partly by their concentration on the positive process of helping people to become involved and achieve goals that would not otherwise be possible. Because we do not represent either authority or threat we are able to develop open and trusting relationships more readily than would be possible if we had first to handle the assumed adversarial nature of the 'manager/worker' relationship. This provides an ideal opportunity for us to question and challenge existing assumptions and to stimulate different, more positive, productive and accurate views.

To be successful facilitators have to understand the likely start point as far as the workforce is concerned, and to recognize that this is a product of traditional views about organizations and management that have held sway for many years, rather than any inherent set of attitudes. Many challenges face the facilitator who is working with the organization as a whole, and it is a tribute to the power of the role that, when it is performed with knowledge, skill and care, it is invariably instrumental in achieving solid and sustained progress.

6 Changing and developing groups

Much of the facilitator's time is spent working with different types of group. These could include problem-solving groups, management teams and boards of directors and so there is a clear need to develop a good working knowledge of at least the basics of what has become known as group dynamics.

The subject of what happens in groups that affects their performance is one of the most intensively researched in the whole field of social psychology and much is known about it. In fact there is so much material and knowledge that it would take a lifetime of study even to scratch the surface. For the practising facilitator who is interested in achieving results within a realistic time period there is a need for an outline of the most important variables that occur in practice, a 'road-map' to help in the diagnosis of what is really happening that is influencing the work of any particular group at any particular time, and some guidelines to help in working on its development. This chapter is designed to meet this requirement.

Groups that meet on a regular basis go through a number of well-defined stages of development. Various researchers have noted this, and it is indisputable. Tuckman proposed that there were four stages which he called Forming, Storming, Norming and Performing. This is a popular description and is well used and memorable. For the practising facilitator, however, it is useful to distinguish between what is happening in the group as far as the relationships of the members are concerned and what is happening on the task front. The idea was put forward by John E. Jones, who also identified four stages of group development, that in many ways parallel Tuckman's.

When a group first comes together, it is characterized on the personal relations front by a phase of dependency. Group members, because they will probably be feeling a little confused and maybe somewhat anxious, will lean on the leader or facilitator to tell them what the ground rules are, to set the agenda and in general to do all of the leading. They will also tend to be quite defensive, and not prepared to take what they see as risks in terms of their behaviour.

On the task side there will at first be a considerable amount of questioning, with members asking why they are there, what they are supposed to do and so on. This phase, which concerns orientation, does not necessarily last for long but it has to be recognized and we should be clear about what is happening during it since it is, clearly, not a very productive period and needs to be worked through as quickly as possible. This stage broadly equates with Tuckman's 'forming'.

The second phase consists of much negative activity since this is the period of conflict. In terms of the relations between group members, as people become more confident of themselves, they start to bring out their own personal agendas. At this stage there will quite possibly be challenges to the leadership of the group, people will criticize negatively and question the motives of others in the group. At this stage as well, some members may try to use the group as a platform for some of their own personal whims and so take the group away from its real task. Often the conflict is hidden, some members may withdraw for example, but the conflict is always there and needs to be seen for what it is, a phase to be worked through.

On the task side the second stage is one where the group

begins to become organized. Questions are raised about such issues as who will be responsible for what, what if any are the rules and boundaries of the task and the authority of the group. These issues all have the potential for generating more interpersonal conflict which again has to be worked through before the group can move on to the next stage of its development. This is the 'storming' phase in Tuckman's model.

Once the group has worked through whatever issues are raised in this stage it can move on to phase three which fortunately is altogether more productive. On the interpersonal relations front stage three is achieving cohesion. Group members feel good at having resolved the conflicts and they experience a feeling of togetherness which is both comfortable and rewarding from the point of view of the relationships within the group.

This, on the task side, means that people are more willing to be open, to share information and to work together productively on the task, which is obviously a good thing. At this stage, however, members often feel so good about being a part of the group that they drift away from a concentration on the task because their needs for being a part of a cohesive team are being met, and this is enough to keep them together.

We have all come across, and may indeed have been a part of, groups that continue to meet, feel very positive about themselves, and yet seem to produce nothing. It is obviously important that the facilitator keeps a watchful eye open for any evidence of this, because the members of the group may well be enjoying themselves so much that they either do not spot it or are unwilling to do anything about it. Despite this danger groups usually do good work during this phase since much of the negative 'baggage' that prevents progress in the early stages has been worked through, and members are willing to work together for the sake of the group, rather than simply seeing things from their own individual points of view.

The final phase is one that is not reached by many, but it should be the goal of any facilitator to help the group achieve it, since at this stage the group will be performing optimally both on the interpersonal relations and the task fronts. On the relations side stage four consists of real interdependence, where members are committed to the team and its goals rather than their own. People will be comfortable working in whatever way helps most, either individually, in subgroups or as a complete unit.

In these circumstances the concentration of the group on the task side is on real problem-solving. There will be an appetite for trying out new approaches that may help to achieve the task more effectively, and these will not be contaminated by any personal agendas.

If facilitators know about the predictable phases that groups go through, they will be able to see more clearly what is happening during meetings, and will be able to guide the leader and the members through all the different stages. This may well include explaining to the group that there are these understandable and predictable steps. In addition it is often necessary to work hard at keeping the group positive and motivated during the early stages which are often uncomfortable and can be demoralising.

It will be in the best interests of both the facilitator and the group to work through the initial two stages as quickly as possible, and this is achieved most effectively by encouragement to address the issues rather than what most untrained people do, which is to try to suppress them. The facilitator should be on the lookout for signs of emerging questioning and conflict and, having briefed the leader on the inevitability of this stage, should play a part in getting members to express their concerns openly. At this time the leader must show a willingness, indeed an appetite, for having his or her views and role questioned since this will help to establish a norm of open, honest communication as well as assisting in working through this phase of the group's development quickly and with the minimum of pain.

The next level of understanding of groups that the facilitator needs, concerns the balance of the group in the sense of the roles that different members take on. We have all had experience of the way that people behave in groups, and how they make different contributions. Some are good at generating ideas, whereas others are more procedural, keeping the group on track. Many people have studied the subject and it is clear that there are a number of well-researched 'team roles'. Belbin's work on this subject is immensely valuable to us, and has already been mentioned in the chapter on understanding groups.

Practising facilitators need to understand the idea of team roles, be able to diagnose what roles are being played within a group, and what effect any imbalances are having. Furthermore we need to be able to help groups create a more effective blend of team roles where this is not currently the case. Since people can develop new roles the facilitator should be able to work with the leader and members of the group to correct or accommodate any roles that are missing, and this is an important part of our role since the effect of a seriously unbalanced team on performance can be very severe.

Belbin's initial studies into the workings of effective and ineffective groups took place over a number of years while he was working at the Management College at Henley-on-Thames, which is well known for its use of the syndicate method of training. As a result of his work he identified eight different team roles. He found, for example, that the most creative people are highly imaginative and experimental, intelligent and assertive, but that a group made up entirely of such people, far from being ideal, tends to be ineffective. He explained this as being because such people tend to be unsympathetic to the methods that have to be employed by administrators to get things done. Such people, 'plants' in Belbin's terminology, for all their strengths, often tend to be impractical and indecisive.

In an effective group the more feasible ideas are identified and translated into action by implementers, called 'company workers', whose main skills are in achieving targets and getting results through people. 'Company workers' are tough-minded, practical, conservative, trusting, conscientious and controlled. An effective group also needs an intelligent, shrewd and serious-minded person to judge the ideas generated by the 'plant', a role called the 'monitor/evaluator'.

Other roles found in effective groups include that of the 'completer/finisher' who is primarily concerned with high standards and the completion of schedules. Next there is the 'resource investigator' who is good at identifying and contacting external sources of help. The sixth role is that of the 'team worker' who helps to defuse difficult situations that occur in the group. Then there is the role of 'chairperson' who is concerned for objectives, strategies, policies and organization, and is good at delegating. This person is able to take a more detached view and see things from the perspective of the organization rather than getting dragged into parochialism. The final role is that of 'shaper', the person who pressurizes, challenges and finds a way round difficulties. 'Shapers' tend to be quite highly strung and can be provoked into angry exchanges at times.

In working with groups the facilitator needs to be able to identify typical behaviours associated with the different roles, and some clues to this are given below. It is also possible to get members to identify their preferences as an activity in its own right by using the questionnaire that Belbin developed and included in his book (Belbin, 1981). This is to be recommended, especially for groups that will meet regularly over an extended period of time since it will help the group to be able to understand much of what happens during their meetings and will give them some ideas for their own development both as individuals and as a team. For the facilitator, however, typical comments which indicate team role preferences are as follows:

- *Chairperson*
  'What we are here to do is . . .'
  'Let's do this first and then move on to that.'
  'To summarize, the main points seem to be . . .'
  'To get back to the main issue . . .'
- *Shaper*
  'What we have to do is . . .'
  'We're wasting time, we should . . .'
  'No, you're wrong, the main issue is . . .'
  'If we put what you have said with the other suggestion we can . . .'
- *Plant*
  'What about . . .'
  'Turning that on its head gives us . . .'
  'A good idea would be . . .'

'Let's look at it from a different angle'
- *Monitor/evaluator*
  'We have to watch out for . . .'
  'Let's not overlook . . .'
  'The problem with that is . . .'
  'This is telling us that we should . . .'
- *Company worker*
  'Let's get this up on the flip chart.'
  'We could do that within our budget.'
  'Given the time we've got we could . . .'
  'If we do that we would be getting nearer to the result.'
- *Resource investigator*
  'What a great idea.'
  'I know someone who can.'
  'Don't worry, I can get them.'
  'I can talk to them and put our point of view.'
- *Team worker*
  'There's no need to fight about it.'
  'Let's listen to Fred's idea.'
  'Why don't you explain that a bit more?'
  'Let's build on Sally's idea.'
- *Completer/finisher*
  'You can't do that, we'll be a week late.'
  'Let me check that.'
  'What about article 3 in subparagraph iv of the second volume?'
  'We have to do this if the whole thing is going to work.'

If the Belbin questionnaire has been used, the facilitator will be aware, not only of the main roles that individual members play, but also their secondary preferences. Armed with this knowledge we can encourage people to spend more time developing the particular secondary roles that will help the overall balance of the group. Where this is done it is important that due recognition is given to those involved, which will, in its turn, encourage the continuation of the behaviour.

Thus far we have looked at the stages groups go through and the team roles that need to be in evidence if the group is to work effectively. Since most groups exist, in one way or another, to make decisions, the subject of decision-making style is the next important topic for the facilitator to be clear about. There are many different ways for a group to come to a decision, and they all have their advantages and disadvantages. Certainly the commitment of members will be affected by the method used and so it is important that groups make conscious choices in the full knowledge of the likely consequences.

The first method, and the one that most groups will intuitively use if they do not know better, is voting. This method does have its place, specifically in situations where there is a very real time constraint and the group is deadlocked. Voting has the advantage of being very quick, but has the serious disadvantage that it invariably creates a dissatisfied minority who are not committed to the decision, and whose motivation for remaining in the group may well be affected, and so it should only be used when there is no other way of the group achieving a decision within the time available.

The second possibility is compromise. This method should not be confused with consensus which is dealt with later. A compromise is an attempt to gain agreement to a decision by a process of trading off the suggestions of different people. It involves all the parties giving up elements of their proposals in an attempt to find a possibility that all parties are prepared to live with even though it is probably far from ideal. In fact, by definition it will never be the ideal solution, and very often it will be rather unsatisfactory for all concerned. Traditional negotiations between management and trade unions tend to be compromises.

As far as groups are concerned the problem with this approach is that it indicates that people are working as individuals rather than as a cohesive single entity. Compromise decisions are usually the 'least worst' decisions rather than the best ones, and so this method should also be avoided wherever possible. Unfortunately, however, many people think in these terms, and even believe that this way of doing things is either good, or inevitable, so the facilitator needs to be on the lookout for it, and to advise that there are alternative approaches, if it seems to be creeping in to the working of the group.

The third decision-making possibility could be called the 'loudest voice' method. Many decisions in organizations are in fact made in this way, not necessarily by the person with literally the loudest voice, but the one with the most perceived power. It is obvious that this option will do nothing to enhance the motivation and commitment of the other members and so should be avoided despite its advantage of being quick and clear, and also its popularity among those with loud voices!

Fourth, there is the 'consensus of silence', which is both insidious and all too common. This happens when someone in the group makes a proposal and then asks other members what they think of it. When no one responds, the silence is taken as agreement, when in fact it could have been that no one was really listening, or that members were worried about causing conflict by disagreeing, or that people were rendered speechless that anyone could suggest anything so stupid! Again it is vital for the facilitator to be on the lookout for this and to help the group confront it if it seems to be happening.

Finally there is the consensus method of making decisions, which is the optimum approach in most circumstances since it represents the best possible result from that group, and also because it maximizes the commitment of group members. The disadvantages of this method are that it is difficult to achieve and that it takes time, which is not always available, but it is infinitely superior to any other method in the quality of the output, so facilitators need to understand consensus, and to help groups to work towards it wherever possible. The difference with consensus is that the decision combines and reflects the best efforts of the whole group, rather than those of one or two individuals. It is positively the best result that can be achieved by the group as a whole and is the decision that all members are prepared to commit themselves to.

We should recognize that consensus does not necessarily mean unanimity. In working for consensus people should avoid arguing only for their own preference, since a true consensus reflects the views of every member of the group. In using this approach it is important to tackle the task in a logical and objective manner but also to recognize that intuitions and feelings have a part to play and should be seen as potentially valuable contributions. Being 'logical and objective' does not mean being sterile and unimaginative. Support should only be given to suggestions with which members are able to agree at least in part, and people should not change their minds only to reach an agreement and avoid conflict. With this in mind differences of opinion should be viewed as a help rather than as a hindrance to the process of making a good decision, and conflict-reducing techniques such as averaging, trading concessions or voting should be avoided.

It should be said that many groups find this process difficult, drawn out and frustrating at times, but for all this it is worth while both in terms of the quality of the decision and the commitment of the members to it, which is why it is the preferred decision-making method wherever possible. Facilitators need to have a thorough understanding of consensus and how it can be achieved, and must be sympathetic to any frustration that this decision-making method provokes. We should stress the benefit of achieving a result that combines and takes into account the best efforts and ideas of everybody. This must be better than a decision which, though quick, does not carry the full support and commitment of all group members.

If the group appears to become frustrated, a useful tactic for the facilitator is to make the point that many problems in organizations reappear because they have not really been solved properly, and that one of the main reasons for this is that members rush at the issue and take the first, seemingly obvious solution, rather than spending a little more time and ensuring that the issue is confronted rigorously. Furthermore, if the group wants to achieve the recognition that is so important to all of us, we will be best served by an approach which, though it takes a little longer in some instances, will guarantee the best possible result from that group. The purpose of establishing the group is to solve the problem, and to make sure that it stays solved, and to spend as much time as is necessary to ensure this. Any time pressure that is felt by the group is likely to be self-inflicted, and facilitators need to have the skills to make this point in a positive way where necessary.

As has already been said, the subject of groups and their dynamics is a vast one that we could not possibly do full justice to in a book such as this, but there are a number of further issues that need to be dealt with to give facilitators enough basic knowledge to begin to fulfil their role with groups adequately.

When President John F. Kennedy asked 'How could we have been so stupid?' after the disastrous Bay of Pigs invasion, it prompted Irving L. Janis, a well-known researcher into groups and group behaviour, to begin to explore this and other fiascos in American foreign policy, such as the Korean war stalemate and the escalation of the Vietnam war. His work led him to the development of what he called 'groupthink' as a way of explaining the behaviour of such groups as they went about their work. He soon began to realize as well, that the phenomenon was not confined to political groups, but went a long way to explaining some of the phenomena that occur whenever groups meet.

Janis put forward a number of explanations for the bizarre behaviours he was studying. First there is the issue of social pressure. It is well known that members of cohesive groups tend to exert a tremendous amount of pressure on anyone within the group who voices objections to what otherwise appears to be a consensus. This makes it very difficult for the person concerned to do anything other than back down.

Second there is the tendency to develop group norms that are more concerned with keeping group members motivated and happy than with thinking critically and effectively. This applies even when the preferred course of action chosen by the group is clearly going wrong in a big way. People in groups that are exhibiting symptoms of groupthink tend to soft pedal when it comes to criticizing suggestions from other group members because they are more concerned with keeping the group happy and content with itself than with taking the personal risks associated with confrontation.

Logically as groups meet more and the members get to know each other there should be a consequent increase in openness and a decrease in any fear of recrimination having put forward alternative views. With effective groups this is indeed the case, but when groupthink is in evidence precisely the opposite occurs as members suppress thoughts or suggestions that are at odds with the prevailing view of the rest of the group. Unfortunately this phenomenon is very common and can be explained in two ways. First it is a subconscious attempt to avoid destroying the existing unity and second it is based on a commitment to the group which leads people to believe that the view of the majority of this group must be right.

It is worth pointing out that this is not normally done deliberately to avoid criticism, rather it tends to reflect the real feelings of members of such groups to the extent that they do not carry out any of the checks that they would otherwise make before committing themselves to a course of action. In this way private misgivings are rationalized away as being irrelevant or misguided, and so are not aired, and the group continues in the belief that all is well.

Janis uncovered eight symptoms of groupthink:

1 *Invulnerability* Members of such groups tend to share an illusion of invulnerability that serves to deflect them from having to assess the risks that they are taking and provides reassurance that everything will be all right. This feature operates even when the group is presented with clear evidence that would, in other circumstances, cause them at least to rethink their original plan.

2 *Rationalization* Another feature that occurs in groups afflicted with groupthink is their tendency to rationalize their behaviour and to ignore or discredit information that does not support their preferred view. In effect they would rather do anything than reconsider.

3 *Morality* A strong tendency in such groups is to develop a profound belief in the underlying correctness of their moral stance. This belief in themselves as 'the good guys' means that they can safely ignore any moral consequences of their actions.

4 *Stereotyping* People in groups that are the victims of groupthink develop often absurd negative stereotypes of outsiders that are perceived to be in conflict with the aims and ambitions of the group. This 'they are the bad guys' view enables

the group to discount any possible effect that the outsiders might have since they are viewed as being too stupid, weak, or just plain bad for the group to spend any time thinking about them or considering what they might be thinking that could affect the group's plan.

5 *Social pressure* Any member of such a group who does express concerns or doubts will quickly be confronted by other members and brought back into line. People who develop a reputation for doing this may also be made the subject of jokes, again in an attempt to discredit this kind of behaviour.

6 *Self-censorship* Such is the desire to stay within the safe confines of apparent unanimity, that members, even if they have doubts, will often suppress them, saying to themselves that their worries cannot be very important, and that since they must be the only one who is concerned, then it will be in the best interests of the group not to distract the group from its work.

7 *Unanimity* A shared illusion of unanimity is the next symptom. In such groups silence is treated as consent and the assumption is made that anyone who expresses a view which in any way supports the majority is a part of the assumed unanimity. In practice, of course, because doubts and alternative views are being suppressed, there is no real unanimity at all, but the group reinforces anything that seems to indicate that a unanimous view is held.

8 *Mindguards* Mindguards, within the terminology of groupthink, are the people who 'protect' the group from outside information that is counter to the inside view. This helps to avoid the situation of the group having to question the correctness of its stance, which may cause its illusions to be shattered.

It is obvious that a group which lapses into groupthink will not perform well and its decisions will be questionable to say the least, so facilitators will do well to develop their skills at diagnosing when this insidious and all too common phenomenon is in evidence.

To assist in this there are a number of tell-tale signs to be on the lookout for, the first of which is that such groups limit their discussions to a minimum number of possible courses of action, rather than exploring all the possibilities before coming to a decision. Second, such groups never re-examine their preferred course of action even after the risks of their approach have been pointed out, they continue with their blind faith that they must be right. Third, they never reassess rejected options to see if they have missed anything. Fourth, they rarely seek out and listen to expert opinion from outside the group and fifth, they display selective perception, showing interest in and accepting evidence that supports their view and ignoring and discounting evidence that is contrary to it. Finally, such groups never think through how their preferred course might be derailed by any of the myriad things that could possibly go wrong, in other words they do not undertake any contingency planning, preferring to exist in the belief that they are inviolable.

Facilitators will of course be anxious to avoid any groups they are working with from falling into these traps and Janis gives a number of guidelines to help achieve this:

1   Give someone the job of critical evaluator or devil's advocate to make sure that doubts and objections are aired. Ensure that the leader is willing to have his or her views criticized just the same as the rest of the group.
2   Avoid members of the group, especially important ones, taking fixed stances from the outset, rather get them to take an impartial position at the beginning. Encourage the airing of alternative possibilities.
3   If the issue is important enough, set up more than one group to investigate it.
4   Gather in outside views from other people in the organization, or experts in the particular field being discussed and make sure they are listened to carefully.
5   If the subject under review involves outsiders, spend time thinking about things from the other point of view.
6   Be prepared to divide into subgroups to force the development of alternative scenarios that the whole group then discusses.

7   Having reached a preliminary consensus, have every member in turn express any residual doubts or objections in as vivid a way as possible, so giving the group the chance to reconsider before coming to its final proposal.

These guidelines should be very much in the forefront of the facilitator's mind in working with groups, and every encouragement should be given to use them both routinely and rigorously if groupthink is to be avoided.

Strangely, one of the most important issues that the facilitator must be aware of when working with groups concerns the management of agreement rather than the management of disagreement or conflict. This may sound odd, but it is an important dynamic that is explained by Gerry Harvey's 'Abilene Paradox'.

Harvey was sitting with his wife and parents on their veranda on a sweltering summer's day. There was nothing particular to do. All of a sudden the father said 'why don't we go into Abilene and get an ice-cream and a nice cold Coke?' Now Abilene was 200 miles away, it was nearly 100 degrees and the car had no air conditioning. The mother replied, hesitatingly, that it sounded like a good idea if he wanted to. The wife said that she supposed there was nothing else to do, and Harvey himself said that he would go along with what everyone else said that they wanted to do. They all got into the car, not noticing the look of slight mortification in the father, who had suggested the idea in the first place.

They struggled into Abilene, had their ice-cream and Coke, struggled back and arrived home hot, sticky and not in the best of moods; the atmosphere amongst them was not good. Harvey then said, more out of frustration than anything, 'Why did we do that?' The mother's response was that father wanted to and that though she didn't want to go herself, she was supporting her husband. The wife said that she certainly did not want to go, but that she had no better suggestion, Harvey said that he did not want to spoil everybody else's enjoyment even though he thought that it was a crazy idea. They all looked at the father who said that he didn't really want to go, but that no one was saying anything at the time and that he was just making conversation!

So four sane, intelligent people, under no apparent duress, had driven 400 miles in extreme heat, with no air-conditioning even though none of them wanted to do it. There was no disagreement, they had failed to manage the fact that they actually agreed that it was a crazy idea.

Eleven years ago I was running my business from my house, a small but very lovely old building. My wife and I decided that we needed a bigger place so that we could separate the business from our private lives. We looked around and eventually found a place that was certainly big. It had a wing that would be ideal to run the business from. It was a barn that had been converted, badly; there was a big hole in the roof, the wooden cladding was rotten, the windows did not fit properly, the plaster was falling off the walls, the kitchen was a disgrace, all in all it resembled a not very well looked after pigsty. We bought it and moved in.

It was not until many months, and many tears, later that my wife suddenly said, 'Why did we do this, we moved from our lovely little cottage to a place we both hate, it's crazy!' I replied, honestly, 'But you said that you wanted it, I could never understand why, but you said you wanted it.' She said, 'I only said that because you said you wanted it!' I said, 'I only said that because you said you wanted it!' To this day our private name for the place is Abilene, and when making decisions together we always try to check them by asking each other, 'Are we going to Abilene?'

The point is that we were unsuccessful in managing the fact that we did in fact agree, and we had done something that neither of us wanted. Since this is such a common phenomenon facilitators need to be aware of it and constantly to be on the lookout for indications that it may be happening in the groups that they are working with. This is achieved by having group members give alternative suggestions before any decision is made, encouraging them to think through the consequences of the proposal, to air any doubts that they have in a non-judgemental way, and finally to say, if they can, why the proposal is a good idea in their own terms not anyone else's.

So far in this chapter we have dealt with important aspects in understanding groups from the point of view of the dynamics of the group as a whole. We also need to be able to take into account the influence that individual behaviour has on the performance of a group, since one of the important roles of facilitators is to be able to diagnose situations where individual behaviour is not helping the group to work effectively.

We can consider the important influences that individuals have on group process under six main headings.

Activity level

In any group there will be those that are more actively involved than others; some seem to talk most of the time whereas others are quieter. Often the balance changes during a meeting, and there is always a reason for this. In many groups it seems to be up to one or two individuals to keep the group moving forward, and we need to know why this is so and what effect it is having on the group. There is nothing intrinsically wrong with there being high and low participators in a group, as long as no one is being excluded and as long as there are members of the group fulfilling the so-called 'gatekeeping' role and helping people to get into the discussion if they want to. A problem which sometimes occurs in groups, however, is that some people fulfil a 'gateclosing' role, shutting group members out. Where this happens, and it can happen subtly, it is obviously vital to diagnose and correct it quickly.

The key questions about individual levels of participation are, therefore:

1   Are the more active participants monopolizing the discussion?
2   Is anyone who could make a useful contribution being excluded?
3   Is enough work being done to encourage quieter members to contribute? Often they are the ones who have the greatest insight, because they have listened to all the contributions to date.

Kinds of influence

Level of participation is not the same as influence. Quite often people who talk a great deal are not really listened to, and have very little influence over other group members, and vice versa. This is an important part of the process, as is the method of influencing the group. Some people try to force their own opinions on others regardless of their views, which is called self-authorized behaviour. Other people prefer a democratic style and want to ensure that everyone has a say. Some individuals try to influence the group by refusing to be drawn in, and this kind of negative influence can obviously have a serious effect on the group as a whole.

The key questions here, then are:

1　Who are the influential group members?
2　Why is this? Is it because of their knowledge of the subject or for other reasons? What are the other reasons?
3　What styles of influence are used in the group? Which are accepted and which are rejected by other members?
4　Do the styles of influence of dominant members fit in with the desire and expectation of the rest of the group, or is a win/lose relationship developing between different people on the basis of the method being used to try to influence the rest?

Defensiveness

We all use defence mechanisms to avoid having to come to terms with what is really happening. Sometimes they are used consciously, but often they operate at an unconscious level. The latter are difficult to treat, since there is a likelihood that any feedback of a direct kind will be rejected. None the less, they have a serious effect on the work of groups and need to be understood.

Defence mechanisms apply to individuals and to groups. As far as individuals are concerned the most common that facilitators need to understand and be able to deal with are the following:

1   *Rationalization*   Someone substitutes an invalid reason for the real one, to avoid either consciously or unconsciously having to cope with the implications of the real reason. An example could be, 'The reason the presentation went badly was that the projector bulb broke', rather than, 'We didn't have a spare bulb and we didn't perform very well'. Another example could be, 'The reason the group performed badly was that my members were not capable of the task', rather than, 'I did not lead, train and motivate them well enough'.

2   *Withdrawal*   A physical symptom of this mechanism often occurs when someone moves his or her chair back, or sits back in their chair. Some people leave groups because they feel they cannot deal with what is happening; and where this happens, it is also a defence mechanism. Obviously there are other reasons for leaving a group as well, so it is not possible to say that anyone who leaves is behaving defensively. Other symptoms of withdrawal are boredom and refusal to enter into the work of the group.

3   *Cynicism*   Usually made manifest by questioning whether the work being done is worth while. Someone who says, 'It's not worth it, they'll just say no eventually' could be really saying, 'I'm not sure I can cope with this way of working'.

4   *Generalization*   The tendency to make generalized statements about what is happening, or what has happened, rather than being specific. Someone who was very worried about playing a part in a management presentation could say, 'I'm not sure presentations should be a part of our work because people can get quite worried about them'.

5   *Competition*   Competition within the group is a relatively common phenomenon, as is competing with the leader or facilitator. Inappropriate competition has its roots in win/lose and often is a way of people saying to themselves, 'No one could blame me for what is happening; it's all their fault!'

As has been said, we are all defensive. No one should be allowed to feel flawed or demeaned by the assumption that we all need defence mechanisms. There are times, however, when they are counter-productive and need dealing with. In diagnosing counter-productive defensiveness the facilitator will need to put the visible behaviour into the wider context of the meetings, and the possible threats that any group member might feel. The key questions here include:

1　Is this truly what the member of the group wanted to say or do?
2　If defensiveness is indicated, is it detrimental to the progress being made by the group? If not, leave it alone.

Achieving the task

Within any group someone must ensure that tasks are achieved and that the group remains on target. There is no point in having a very happy group that has enjoyable meetings and yet achieves nothing. There are a number of different requirements here, from making sure that the problem-solving structure is appropriate, to keeping the group on target and concentrating on the task at hand. Often there will be more than one person in the group who fulfils roles like these, and this is fine as long as no role conflict is generated.

Key questions regarding this problem include:

1　Is anyone keeping the facts and the discussion updated and in front of the group by summarizing the situation to date?
2　Is anyone ensuring that all the relevant data, whether they be facts, opinions or alternative solutions, are being collected?
3　Is someone making sure that the problem-solving structure being used is suitable for the task?
4　Do members keep moving from one subject to another, thus stopping the group from making progress down its chosen path?

Some aspects of group dynamics, of course, are affected by the whole group or subgroups rather than individuals, and it is to the most important of these that we shall now turn.

Atmosphere

That groups have an atmosphere would be readily accepted by most people who have ever been in one. Equally there would be widespread agreement that the kind of atmosphere can have an important effect on the group concerned. Because of this the facilitator will want to get a sense of the atmosphere and what is affecting it. Some groups fall into the habit of having congenial meetings, where everyone gets on well and yet nothing gets done. Others are cold and clinical, and not necessarily any more effective. The atmosphere in a group will spring from many causes, and the questions to ask include:

1 What effect are the physical surroundings having?
2 What effect is the task the group is engaged in having?
3 To what extent do members feel able to make contributions without fear of being made to look foolish or being ignored?
4 What is the leader's contribution to the atmosphere in the group?
5 How much of the business of the group seems to be done above the table and how much under it?

Subgrouping

A potentially dangerous possibility that will certainly affect the morale and effectiveness of the group is subgrouping. This can occur for a number of reasons, and almost invariably leads to the formation of 'in groups' and 'out groups', which can so easily lead the group itself into an unproductive and debilitating win/lose situation. Subgrouping is relatively easy to diagnose although the underlying motivations of the participants may not be clear. We should be careful not to overreact where subgroups are formed, especially if they are 'one off' events. It is when they start to become habitual, with the same 'in groups' and 'out groups', that the situation needs to be dealt with.

Key questions to ask in diagnosing serious subgrouping include:

1   Is there any consistent agreement or disagreement between subgroups?
2   Is there an élite within the group? If so, how does it treat the rest of the group?
3   Is there a subgroup which is vying for leadership of the group? If so, is there one individual behind it?
4   Do the same subgroups always form over the same issues: for example, the choice of problem to be tackled next, finger-pointing at other departments, or organizing roles for the management presentations?
5   Are the subgroups helping or hindering the group as a whole? Is the whole group in control of this aspect of its process, and can it cope with the implications?
6   Is there any straightforward 'ganging up'? If so, urgent action is needed.

Group rules

Any group which meets on a regular basis develops rules that members abide by. These rules, or norms as they are usually called, are often unspoken, and yet they are inviolable for any-one who wishes to continue as a member. Sometimes a norm will only be recognized by some of the members, and occasionally it can happen that no one is really aware of some of the prevailing 'rules' even though they have an important impact on what is and is not acceptable behaviour within the group.

One of the first issues that group members should address is to establish the positive 'norms' that they wish to abide by in their meetings. An example of an 'open' norm that many effective groups choose to make explicit is that there should be no nega-tive criticism of any idea that is brought up at the meeting.

Clearly facilitators will want to be sure that they have a good idea of what the important norms are, first, so that they do not violate them themselves, and second, so that they can better understand the behaviour of the particular group.

Important diagnostic questions here include:

1   What are the explicit rules that members agree to abide by?
2   What sanctions does the group impose on members who transgress? Are the sanctions counter-productive?
3   What seem to be the unspoken rules? Would it help the group to make them explicit? Sometimes the answer to this question is a definite 'no'. We should not automatically think that openness is a good thing.
4   Are there any subjects that seem to be taboo? Does this materially affect the work of the group?
5   Do any of the unspoken norms seem to contravene any of the core principles of effective group working?
6   Are there any norms to do with the expression of the feelings of group members? Being able to express feelings is an important part of being an effective group. If this is taboo, something will probably need to be done.

This section is not intended to be a comprehensive treatment of group process. That would take an encyclopaedia. What it attempts to do is to highlight aspects of the subject which are likely to have practical value to the facilitator of different types of group.

There are many books and articles on group working and group process (*see* Sources and Resources at the end of this book). It is a subject with a fascination all of its own, where it is almost impossible to lay down hard and fast rules and yet where there are so many generalizations that always seem to come true. It is also a subject, fortunately or unfortunately, where the more one learns, the more one realizes how little one knows. There is no doubt that for the practising facilitator to be success-ful, a working knowledge of group process is required and for many the study of groups becomes an ongoing obsession. This chapter is designed to give a basic understanding of enough dimensions of the subject to be able to work with groups success-fully and to be able to give them clear and coherent advice when needed.

7 Changing and developing individuals

Very recently a rather new way of looking at the context within which we are trying to create successful change has been developed. It is interesting and important enough in dealing with individuals to warrant inclusion here since it reveals a new dimension of the development process that we cannot afford to ignore.

Economic history textbooks tell us about the Industrial Revolution. They explain in intricate detail the changes that transformed us from a society based on agriculture and cottage industry into one that was designed to make best use of the new mass production technologies that were becoming available. Economic historians in the future will look back and see that the Industrial Revolution that started in the latter part of the eighteenth century was actually just the first, and that there have been two more revolutions since then that have impacted all our lives as much, if not more.

If the first concentrated primarily on the deployment of people's arms and legs, the sweat of their brow, the second, which gathered pace in the 1960s and has had an ever-increasing impact since, concerns the use of people's brains. The so-called 'knowledge' industries have mushroomed since that time, and have contributed technologies that mean that much which had to be done by hand in the past can now be mechanized. This is the case with the work done in all functions of the organization, from production, with robotics, to engineering design with CAD/CAM (computer-aided design/computer-aided manufacturing), to accounts and other previously clerical functions with a whole array of customized software tools.

We are all aware that this process continues at an ever-faster rate, and that it is not going to stop. Partly because of this and also because of the increasing realization of some of the effects of the first two revolutions, there is an increasing awareness of the third, the Emotional Revolution. This recognizes that the people who make up the workforce of all our organizations from top to bottom, bring more than muscle and brainpower with them to work; they also bring a complex set of emotions that have just as great an impact on what happens and does not happen, what works and what does not work. This recognition represents the greatest challenge for the management and leadership of organizations today and into the future.

Powerful though the new technologies are there was, and still is, a big danger of falling into just the same trap as did Taylor in thinking that people could be deployed on the assumption that they would always behave rationally when presented with a logical reason for a course of action, whereas we all know that this is not necessarily the case. Applying this understanding quite literally transforms our perception of the managerial role, and places much greater demands on the ability of the manager to be able to respond appropriately and successfully to the situation that presents itself. Facilitators in being aware of this can be of great assistance to others in developing their understanding and their ability to handle it successfully.

For an example of this we can look at the airline industry, which has transformed itself over the past few years. Historically the belief was that the job of the airline was to get us to our destination and that was about it. Some people were needed in the cabin to provide, usually disgusting, food to the passengers, to serve them drinks when the staff felt like it, and to be generally imperious and condescending. The important part of the job was being done at the front, by the pilot, who had a comprehensive 'manual' to refer to. It could all be done 'by numbers'. This was the case for years, but then a few years ago, the airline companies were progressively forced to recognize that they were missing a number of important points to do with the psychological make-up of their customers. Those that didn't either went out of business or will.

The fact is that when we board an aeroplane we make the basic assumption that it is going to arrive; if we didn't believe this, we would not board the plane in the first place. So while we are travelling, we are not constantly wondering whether we will arrive at the destination, we are much more concerned with how we are being treated in the process. Simple enough, we may say, just encourage the cabin staff to smile at people and say 'have a nice day'; add in more decent food and that should do the trick! It also has the advantage that you can write it all down in a manual so there's no excuse for anyone not doing it. Of course, though, arguably, an improvement, this approach is just as flawed as the first.

On a jumbo jet that is being boarded at this minute there are some people who are going on holiday, some are going to weddings, others to funerals. There are those that are frightened of flying and there are seasoned business travellers. Some will become drunk and be jolly, others will become drunk and be morose and difficult. Some will have expectations of being personally looked after every minute of the way and others will just want to be left alone. And so it goes on; that plane represents a microcosm of almost every dimension of life. The pilot is at the front and, we assume, will deliver us to the destination safely, but in the meantime the cabin staff have to deal with us.

Where is the manual that can cover each and every eventuality in this situation? Of course there isn't one; if there were it would probably take up the whole plane, and would still be a trivialization of the true requirement. The situation is that with some basic training and some ground rules which reflect the philosophy of the airline company, the cabin staff have to use their skill, intuition, perceptiveness and luck in an attempt to satisfy every passenger. Whether they or we like it or not, they have to deal, not only with the rational part of humankind, but also the emotional part, and it is often the emotional part, however irrational, that holds sway. The best and most successful cabin staff will be those that recognize this and have the motivation, skills and flexibility to deal with the different circumstances in different and appropriate ways. Those who try to 'do it by numbers' will succeed some of the time, but not very often. The best that they can hope for is that they will escape without causing too much damage.

This is a specific example from a particular industry, but we could create equivalent examples for every organization. The management role is to achieve the best out of the resources that are being used, and without the ability to handle the emotional content that people bring with them to work, it is hard to see how this can be achieved. So the third Industrial Revolution presents us with a different challenge that cannot be reduced to a set of rules and regulations, but which requires the ability of the manager or facilitator to understand what is happening from the point of view of the other person, and to have enough skill to deal with it flexibly and proactively.

Historically we have not trained our managers to be able to understand this, let alone deal with it, and yet we know today that what we are describing here represents well over 90 per cent of most managers' jobs. Unless we can accommodate this reality we will not be able to manage change in anything but a random and haphazard manner, or one that is mechanical and procedural, and therefore so trivialized as to be unworthy of comment.

So the lesson of the third Industrial Revolution is that we are indeed dealing with 'complete' human beings in the work that we do, and that we had better understand this, accept it and value it if we wish to make progress in creating successful change. We cannot alter the fact that all human beings have their quirks and sometimes behave in the strangest of ways, ways that sometimes defy belief! The complexity of dealing with this is made greater by people's natural tendency to justify what they do, an issue dealt with in detail, during the discussion on attitudes that can be found elsewhere in this chapter.

These two factors affect the task of the change agent profoundly, and since we cannot alter them we need to develop the necessary skills and flexibility to deal with them effectively. This argues strongly for the development of a bedrock of knowledge about human behaviour and its dynamics, that is so well entrenched that it can be accessed and used at will, in whatever circumstance the facilitator is placed.

In working with our customers, we are primarily concerned with achieving improvement. Improvement, by definition, involves change, which means not continuing to do things in the same way as in the past, but taking on board new behaviours. All of this is, of course, obvious, but its implications are vitally important for anyone who wants to be an effective facilitator. Most people are very defensive when it comes to their own behaviour and the opportunities that exist for improvement. We are all very adept at seeing how others can improve, but when it comes to our own behaviour the issues tend not to be so clear to us, and there are always very good reasons to explain away what has happened. We tend to see the opportunity for improvement as a negative comment on our current behaviour and so we become defensive.

One of the main reasons for the remarkable transformation of Japan since the Second World War is that they have a concept called 'Kaizen' which permeates their culture. The nearest translation of the word Kaizen is continuous improvement, the idea that everything can and should be improved, not necessarily by quantum leaps, more by a whole series of small steps. Because the Japanese are brought up with this idea, they are not defensive about change and improvement, in fact they value it and enjoy it.

It is this attitude that we, as facilitators, are trying to engender in our customers; a searching for, and enjoyment of, positive and beneficial change in our own behaviour. If we can achieve this, a continuous drive to personal improvement in our customers, and of course ourselves, we will have contributed much to the well-being of ourselves, those we are working with and the organizations within which they work. For us to be able to work toward this goal in a coherent and systematic way we need to understand what attitudes are and the process by which they change, since it is a change in attitude that we are, for the most part, trying to achieve.

It is odd that for a word so often used, there is so little real understanding of what an attitude is and still less about the process by which they change. Yet the subject of attitudes is one of the best researched in the whole field of social psychology, much is known about them and the process by which they change. It is not too extreme to say that the whole field of social psychology is, in fact, the systematic study of attitudes.

An attitude is 'a predisposition to act', and contains two important, discrete and definable parts. The first is everything that we know about the subject in question, our database. This is the cognitive element and could be said to include our beliefs, which, however irrational they might be, still form an important part of what we claim is what we know. Second are our feelings about the issue which is called the affective element, so attitudes reflect both our hearts and our heads.

The next thing that we need to know about the subject is that human beings have a very powerful urge to keep the different parts of any particular attitude in balance. This is because it is psychologically very uncomfortable for us to be in a situation where our head is telling us one set of information, and our heart something different and in conflict with the first. Every human being will act to reduce this dissonance and to bring the attitude in question back into balance.

An example of this, which some of us may understand, concerns a married couple who love each other. They have a large amount of knowledge about each other which is positive, and they have warm and affectionate feelings. Then, one day they have a blazing row! The row lasts, individually they begin to feel miserable, they do not want to eat their food, they drink too much. All these are physiological symptoms that none of us wants to continue with. On reflection, during this time the two people realize that although the 'database' in their head is giving them one set of information about their partner, the fact is, at the moment, that they can't stand each other, and the whole situation is intolerable.

So what is the solution? Well, it is to shift their attitudes back into some sort of balance. One way of doing this would be for them to change what they know about each other and bring it in line with their current feelings; the result, divorce; and attitudes in balance, 'I always knew that he/she was a terrible person really'. The other way is to bring their existing feelings back in line with their knowledge base, in other words to 'kiss and make up' and again the result is that their attitudes are back in balance; until the next time! The point is that either way the attitude of both the people concerned will get back in balance. Consider what divorced people do actually say about their previous spouses and you will understand.

In the normal course of events when our attitude to a certain issue is in balance we will not change it, since we do not tend willingly to create the kind of discomfort involved. Yet this is precisely what the facilitator is trying to do, to encourage the customers to be willing to change their attitude about themselves in favour of one that does not rationalize but actively and positively seeks out opportunities for beneficial personal change and improvement, and confronts the issues involved in making them happen. Because this process is at the root of much that the facilitators do, it is obviously of great importance that they understand the process by which attitudes change, and master the skills of helping people to do it.

If we do not change our attitudes while they are in balance, but only when we experience the discomfort when they are out of synchronization, clearly the business of attitude change in some way involves creating a temporary imbalance, in a controlled enough way for the attitude to be adapted in a positive way. Of all the researchers on the subject, Leon Festinger provides us with the most useful and usable theory of attitude change. His Theory of Cognitive Dissonance states that:

If people are induced to say or do something contrary to their private attitude, they will tend to modify their thoughts and feelings [in other words their attitude] to bring them into line with their new behaviour. He adds an important rider, however, which is that the greater the pressure used to bring about the change of attitude [beyond the minimum needed to achieve it], the less the attitude will change.

Festinger explains this process as one of rationalization. We all need to justify our actions, and we spend much of our time doing just that, either out loud or in our minds. Thieves say that those that they steal from can afford it, or that they are not really stealing from people, just insurance companies, and they deserve it anyway! People who have given bad service say that they weren't feeling well, or that the customer was rude to them first. I say that I didn't write the 2 000 words I committed myself to write yesterday because the phone kept ringing rather than because I didn't concentrate on the job in hand and make sure that I completed the work, which of course I could have done. You say, 'I only did it because . . .'.

If I were to offer you a million pounds to jump off a high building, given the certain knowledge that you would not kill yourself, but that you would certainly break a few bones, many of you would do it. Lying in hospital afterwards, with the pile of money in front of you, you need to justify your behaviour, because presumably you do not make a habit of jumping out of windows, I have induced you to do something that is contrary to your private attitude. The most likely justification for this bizarre behaviour will be that you did it for the money. Thus your original attitude remains intact, you do not need to change it because you can say to yourself that it was the pressure, in the form of money, that I put on you that made you do it. You are unlikely to choose to do it again, your original attitude has remained in balance throughout the experience, of course it is stupid to jump off high buildings, but not nearly as stupid as offering a million pounds to do it!

Now take the same scenario, but this time I offer you a hundred pounds, or five hundred, whatever amount is only just enough to elicit the behaviour. As you lie in your hospital bed it is much more difficult for you to justify what you have done in purely money terms, because it was only just enough, and yet you still have, in your mind, to justify yourself. It is at this point that the minimum pressure has been brought to bear to make you act in a way that is outside your normal attitude, and it is at this point that the amount of 'dissonance' is at its greatest. Your attitude to the subject is now vulnerable. Of course you may decide that you made a mistake and retain your existing attitude, but on the other hand you may justify yourself by saying things like 'it is good to test and challenge oneself' or 'I showed that I'm not scared of actions like that' or 'if I had rolled over on landing I wouldn't have injured myself at all!'

The purpose of these examples is to demonstrate the points that Festinger was making about creating maximum dissonance by applying minimum pressure, and the built in need that we all have to justify what we do. If we want one single explanation of so many of the vagaries of human behaviour, then this is it, and anyone who has dealings with people and needs to be able to understand why they behave in the way that they do will do well to take the messages to heart.

Though simple, this theory is of profound importance in understanding human behaviour, and is certainly fundamental to the facilitator role. If too much pressure is brought to bear a change in short-term behaviour will be achieved, but people will revert to their original stance as soon as the pressure is removed. Think of our children. When they are young it is easy for a parent to force a child to do something that he or she does not want to, but does this mean we have changed their attitude? Just wait until our back is turned!

The same sort of things happen countless times in organizations every day; it could be said that a large part of the history of organizational change is the story of people trying to change attitudes with no knowledge of how to do it, and in fact producing short-term behaviour change that did not stand the test of time. Think of all the initiatives that your organization has introduced over the years, and consider how well they lasted. In most organizations many of them faded away after a few months or a year, and became known as the latest in a long list of temporary fads or 'management gimmicks'. All this is explained by Festinger's theory, and could have been avoided with skilful use of the lessons it contains.

As facilitators working at the individual level, we do not want our efforts to suffer the same fate as so many of these organizational initiatives. So what are the implications of the theory for our work?

First we should recognize that the fact that we will not usually have a direct line relationship with our customers, and so will have no real 'power', is in fact a great advantage. The management process in most organizations puts considerable pressure on people. In some instances this is simply pressure to do as they are told whereas in others it is more subtle. At the back of it all as well is the ultimate pressure which is the ability of the organization to fire people. This, understandably, often breeds a sterile and uncommitted conformity, a complete lack of any sort of 'ownership' and an attitude of 'it's nothing to do with me, I just do as I'm told'. Because we as facilitators do not have this kind of authority over those we are working with, we can, with skill, transform this kind of negative stance into something much more positive and beneficial for all.

The second important implication is that in helping people to change their attitudes we are involved in deliberately trying to create a certain discomfort, not out of any desire to cause pain, but as a vital ingredient in the process of development and improvement. Many inexperienced and untrained facilitators seem to believe that all they are there to do is to be pleasant to their customers and to 'stroke' them, whatever they do. This in practice will achieve very little, apart from reinforcing a feeling of comfort that will further entrench the *status quo* rather than acting to improve it. Of course, in creating this feeling of discomfort we have to be careful that we do not apply too much pressure and so end up not creating any dissonance at all, merely demotivating and annoying those that we are working with.

So skill and judgement are required to achieve just the right amount of creative discontent in those that we are working with. This is further complicated by the fact that different amounts will be required for different people, and different strategies will have to be employed depending on the personalities and motivations of those concerned. With some people it will be easier and more appropriate to work on amending their knowledge base, whereas with other people it may be better to work on inserting some new feelings. Either approach if handled well can do the trick, which is to create an imbalance in the person's current attitude which is a necessary prerequisite for attitude change. These are complexities, but they do not change the principle of what it is that we are trying to do.

The third implication for us as facilitators lies in understanding that if we can structure the process successfully, the ownership of the improvements will be firmly with the people that we are dealing with, and that if the result is positive the 'new attitude' will become the normal 'predisposition to act', in other words there will come a point at which the role of facilitator as catalyst will no longer be needed, since the new set of behaviours will be a natural reflection of the newly balanced attitude. At this point the facilitator can move on and work with different people. This is a big advantage since it is not only an effective process, it is also efficient in that it does not require constant and continual input and monitoring. This is also the reason why facilitative styles of line management are increasingly being recognized as the way of the future, as can be seen in Chapter 20.

This subject is necessary for both an understanding of facilitation and our ability to perform the role successfully. Though it is fairly straightforward, once it has been explained, and though in a common sense way it explains so much of what people do and why they do it, it has to be said that applying the knowledge requires a lot of skill which needs practice. As is the case with so much in life, there is much to be said for facilitators applying the learning first to themselves, since it is probable that we, just as much as those that we work with, need to change our own attitudes to ourselves and our own potential for improvement. At the very least we should use Festinger's theory to think through and explain the things that we ourselves do, and consider how we might work with and on ourselves in the cause of our own continuous improvement.

PART III
Facilitator Skills

The facilitator role is a complex one that involves using skills that tend not to be used very well by people in the normal run of events. It is not that the skills are particularly unusual or complicated, rather that we simply do not use them and we certainly do not develop our knowledge and expertise in them. This is rather strange in view of how effective they are, and how much they improve both our performance and that of the people that we are working with, but it is none the less the case.

Any facilitator who wants to be truly effective needs at least a basic toolkit, and over a period of time needs to extend it to be able to be effective in more difficult situations. In this part the basic skills are discussed, as well as some of the more complex ones. Enthusiastic facilitators will find that their development in this area is very much a lifetime journey, and one that will continually bring rewards of greater effectiveness in all of their interactions. The tools covered in the following chapters are to be seen as a starter pack.

It is also worth saying at the outset that although many of the skills covered sound very simple and obvious, they require practice to use successfully, and they require honest and open self-evaluation on the part of the facilitator. To be successful we need to be able to use the skills expertly and with clear objectives in mind. We also need to remember what we did, and be able and honest enough to evaluate our performance accurately.

None of the difficulties we will be dealing with among our customers are their sole preserve; there is an ever-present danger that we will fall into precisely the same traps, and will attempt to rationalize away our behaviour in just the same way that we will see others do as we work with them. To help with this important area of self-assessment a number of diagnostic tools are included to support the content of these chapters. These should be used rigorously until the skills that they explore become second nature. Frankly there is nothing worse than facilitators who do not live by the messages that they are trying to propound.

8   The starting point

Probably the most important general guideline for facilitators is that we must start from where the other person is, and we need to understand precisely why this is so. We also need to appreciate, that, for all its apparent simplicity, this is remarkably difficult to achieve in practice. Facilitators are involved in creating change, helping people to work on improvement activities that otherwise they would not have the motivation, the insight or the time in which to engage themselves. Any such activity needs to start from the current situation, and indeed can start from nowhere else if it is to stand any chance of success.

There was once a cartoon which showed two tramps sitting on a park bench, both 'down and out'. The caption had one of them saying to the other, 'starting from tomorrow I'm going to be a rich and successful person!' The point is, of course, that this was a fantasy that was not going to happen. Two tramps might seem a long way from our own experience, and yet how many of us, at one time or another have said, 'if I won the pools I would be able to . . .', or, 'if I wasn't locked into my domestic situation things would be very different'.

We need to be conscious of any indications from those that we are working with that they are building such fantasies and expecting that the fantasy itself will just happen and will magically create a different starting point. I remember, many years ago, falling into this trap myself. I was a marketing manager at the time, and was having a review meeting with my director who asked me what I wanted. Thinking that I was being clever I said £50 000, which, at the time, would have been enough to have retired on. The director looked at me and said, 'and how do you intend achieving that, Mike, apart from just hoping for eight draws?' The point was well made, and I hope that I learned the lesson.

If the people we are working with need to start from where they are, so do we in the assumptions that we make about their starting point. It is all too easy for us to interpret their present situation in our own terms, and so to miss the point entirely. A while ago my wife told me that she was frustrated that we seemed to be in a rut, cutting ourselves off, and not seeing people. Dutifully I organized some dinner parties to which I invited a range of friends and acquaintances that we had not seen for a time. I even arranged for myself to do the cooking so that she could relax with the guests. The events were fine, but clearly were not addressing the real issue, since the interpretation was that I had organized them in order to show off my prowess in the culinary department. The point, that I had missed, was that she wanted to go out of the house, to some outside events and shows. I had interpreted her starting point in my own terms; I like cooking and dinner parties. This is a small example of a trap that we are always in danger of falling into when working with others, and we need to remind ourselves constantly that we need to be sure that we do understand the situation from the point of view of those we are dealing with, and not 'contaminating' it with our own.

It was Carl Rogers who developed the term and the practice of 'client-centred' therapy. This was based on the notion that, for people to be able to solve their problems, they had first to accept that they had them in their own terms, not just because someone else, however qualified, told them. Then they had to work through their problems and come to their own conclusions if therapy was to have any lasting effect. The role of the therapist in all this was that of a catalyst, who by skilled questioning could keep the person concerned concentrating on the issues at hand rather than drifting off into a series of rationalizations that would not help.

A catalyst in chemistry is something that creates a reaction without itself being changed by it. In the sense that we are using the word here, the therapist causes the change to happen where it would otherwise not, but the precise nature of the change is determined by the client. While Rogers was dealing with people in therapy, facilitators are dealing with people during the normal course of their lives. Furthermore, we are dealing, for the most part, with individuals who are relatively 'healthy' in a psychological sense. None the less we can take much from his stance and can learn from the way he goes about putting it into practice.

While I have been a devotee of Rogers' approach for many years, I believe that there is a danger, for those of us who are not as skilled as he, that in using this method we might appear to be aloof from and 'above' those that we are working with. If this is the perception that we create, it will of course have a profound influence on our effectiveness. I have also come to question the notion of being a catalyst in the pure chemical sense of the word. Over the years of trying to understand things from the point of view of the other party, I have lost count of the number of times when their 'picture of the world' has seemed to make such good sense that it has influenced my own view, and so has 'changed' me. I now believe that accepting this possibility is no bad thing as long as it does not detract or distract from the main objective which is the development of the customer. At least it has helped me to overcome an accusation that used to be levelled at me occasionally, of running experiments using other people's lives.

For the practising facilitator starting at the right point is of paramount importance and so we have to be able to diagnose accurately the mood and mental set of our customer very early in the relationship. This, of course applies equally if we are dealing with individuals or groups. When working with groups the task can be more difficult, since there will be differences between the various members, and furthermore the group itself will have a 'personality' all of its own. This does not alter the requirement for us to work hard and effectively during this diagnostic phase.

Many of the skills that are dealt with in various chapters of this part of the book will be required in order to do this, and different people will approach the task in different ways. As long as we think through our approach carefully this will be better than a prescribed step-by-step procedure, since it will be more natural.

There are a number of core questions that we will want to answer at this early point, however, and these include first, what is the main representational system used by the customer, since this will help us to build rapport if we can match it. Second, we will want to be as clear as we can about the person's 'state', including issues such as whether the indications are of a positive or a negative frame of mind, and does the person appear to be 'OK' or 'not OK' in terms of life position. Third, we will want some clues about how the person concerned views the whole improvement process; is it seen as an opportunity or a threat, an implied criticism or a necessary ingredient for survival and success. Finally, we will want to be able to assess how the person concerned views the facilitator role since we may well have to adapt our own behaviour in the early stages as we work on developing rapport.

However we do it there is no doubt that the whole tenor of the relationship we develop with our customers is likely to be heavily influenced by the first one or two meetings. We will need to listen very carefully to what is said, and what is not said; we will need to work hard to try to see things from their point of view; we will need to find out about their picture of the world, and to probe this so that we can be clear about their attitude on entering this activity. With these issues clear in our minds we will have laid the foundations for the success of those that we are working with, and our own contribution in helping them.

9   Facilitative behaviours

The facilitator role, as we have already mentioned, is concerned with helping people to get things done, to improve their performance and develop themselves in the process. Research indicates that there are a number of generic behaviours that will assist facilitators as they go about this process, and they should become fundamental to the way that facilitators perform their role. The behaviours can be divided into those that are particularly facilitative, and those that are likely to provoke action, which we should constantly remind ourselves is the real purpose of our job.

The first important facilitative behaviour is creating empathy. Without the feeling that the facilitator is 'on the same wavelength' little is likely to be achieved, and the relationship may well deteriorate into a rather sterile, game-playing charade. Empathy breeds a feeling of comfort and confidence that leads in its turn to a greater willingness to be open in both giving and receiving feedback. This is such an important subject that a full chapter is devoted to it, but it is mentioned here as a part of this particular research.

The second ingredient is being specific. It is relatively easy to discuss issues in general terms, people do it all the time, often in an attempt to 'fudge' issues, but this method does not necessarily help very much if our goal is to identify and achieve action on defined improvement opportunities. It is also very difficult to understand the full meaning of generalized statements especially when trying to apply them to developing an understanding of ourselves, and so they tend to frustrate rather than to facilitate. When we are giving feedback it needs to be precise and specific if we want it to facilitate the person we are dealing with.

Genuineness is the third generic behaviour that will help the facilitative process. If the people we are working with doubt our genuineness they will, quite simply, close up and if they are prepared to continue at all, will only do so on the basis of meaningless platitudes. Our genuineness, it is important to note, will be judged in two ways; first, are we seen as being genuinely interested in our customers in their terms, and prepared to work with them on that basis, and second, do we appear to be more interested in our own self-aggrandizement than in the people we are working with. The fact that these judgements will be made on the basis of perceptions that may be erroneous, but will certainly be believed by those who develop them, should alert us to the importance of this issue.

The final particularly facilitative set of behaviours are those that will engender respect. To put it bluntly, it is difficult to imagine such a relationship being fruitful unless this ingredient is present. With no organizational power to fall back on, the success of the role depends on the customer's feeling that it is at least potentially worth their while, and this is only likely to be the case if there is a bedrock of respect in place.

Again we should note that different people respect different things: some think it is clever to be able to drink ten pints of beer without falling over, whereas others are much more impressed with the self-control of the teetotaller. There are, however, some simple general rules that it seems silly to flout. 'Looking the part' does not mean going everywhere in expensive business attire, but it does mean recognizing that first impressions are disproportionately important, and that lasting assumptions will be made on the basis of simple things like appearance, manner, demeanour, politeness and suitable interest and enthusiasm. Furthermore listening carefully to what our customers say will always reveal what they value, which will give us further guidelines as to what to do to develop this most important ingredient.

The other dimension that we are interested in is achieving results, and again there are four sets of behaviours that can help in this, the first of which is concreteness. In trying to help people decide what they want to work on to aid their development, it will not do much good if we are vague and woolly or if we allow them to be the same. In developing action plans with our customers we must help them to define what they intend to do in concrete terms. If we do not, then quite simply the proposed action will never happen, which will do neither party any good.

Second is the issue of immediacy. If an action is agreed to be achieved by the end of the century, then quite understandably it is unlikely to receive a very high priority. It will not happen. The more immediate the requirement, the more likely it is to create action. This does not mean that everything has to be done literally immediately, but actions that are timed at more than approximately a month away will often be lost amongst all the other issues that have to be dealt with, and for many people even a week is a long time. Longer-term plans should be broken down into parts, some of which need to be actioned very quickly to meet the requirement for immediacy.

Inevitably, some of the people with whom we deal will be less willing to commit to actions than others, and so the third issue concerns the ability to confront issues positively and successfully. This needs to be handled in a much more subtle way than it often is if it is going to be successful, but it is essential in many situations, where our customers are either defensive, protective or simply blind to their real situation.

The final behaviour that will help to generate commitment to action is the very powerful one of self-disclosure. It is often the case that people genuinely cannot see the possibilities that face them, or that they are rather frightened by the prospect of a particular course of action. In circumstances such as these it helps a great deal to hear of an equivalent situation that we have found ourselves in, that maybe frightened us, but which we managed to deal with. This will be more powerful the greater the respect that exists, and especially if the example is expressed in a way that imparts an appropriate sense of vulnerability. Of course it will not help if we are dismissive of the difficulty and appear arrogant in the example that we use. It is not always that we can recall a relevant example from our own experience, but it is remarkable how often they are there, and with practice they can be recalled and used to very positive effect.

These behaviours are so important to the effective performance of the facilitator role that it will be well worth while committing them to memory and evaluating the interventions that are made against these criteria.

10 Developing empathy

For the facilitator role to be effective a good and trusting relationship has to be developed with the customer. In fact this needs to be more than just relating to each other well; facilitators have to be able to understand the minds of their customers and to see things through their eyes. The customers for their part need to see and feel that the facilitator understands and relates to them. In other words there needs to be empathy in the relationship.

Many people would claim that such relationships are based on 'chemistry', and that therefore they cannot be created, they are either there or not. This is very far from the truth: there are many skills that we can develop that will help us to build such relationships with any and all of our customers. Some of the skills are simple and fairly obvious and others are still easy to practise, but are not so well-known since they belong to a recent, and still relatively unknown, science called neuro-linguistic programming (NLP).

First, an empathetic relationship is unlikely to be developed unless the facilitator shows an honest interest in the customer. Though obvious it is not always easy to put into practice, especially as many people are a little cautious about the facilitator at the outset mainly because it is new and an unknown quantity. Showing interest needs to be demonstrated physically since it is difficult to see it when it is only expressed within someone's mind. The skills here are simple but effective. Leaning forward when the other person is talking signifies interest, and nodding and saying 'mm' reinforce this perception. This may sound simplistic, but it is not.

Think of a situation that you have been in where you have been convinced that the person you were talking to was not particularly interested in what you were saying, and yet did not say so in words. Now try to remember the other person's body language during the exchange. It is highly likely that you were picking up powerful non-verbal messages, and that it was these that were the cause of your perception. Think also of the judgements that we tend to make on the basis of our interpretation of non-verbal cues.

Be conscious over the next day or so of the number of times you observe such cues and make judgements purely on this basis: most people are very surprised at how often it happens. In the normal course of events we do it almost subliminally and so do not notice, but as facilitators of course we need to be very conscious and aware of such communication.

There is no doubt that for the facilitator the active management of body language is a vitally important skill that must become second nature if empathy is to be developed with our customers, and equally clearly when practising these behaviours we need to be sure that we do not resemble a puppet on a string, with repetitive nodding, and sounding like a record stuck in a groove with constant 'mming! Appropriate and subtle use of the behaviours is the key.

In creating empathy, 'mirroring' is also a very useful skill to develop. We all tend to feel an association with people who look and behave as we do, and mirroring builds on this. It involves, again subtly, echoing the physical positions adopted by the other person. If they are sitting with their legs crossed, echo that; if they have their arm along the back of the chair, echo that, and so on. This sounds very false and some people are concerned that it will be obvious and counter-productive, but done appropriately it is not, and is a genuine way of building rapport. In developing this skill facilitators will need to develop their ability to observe the physical movements of those that they are dealing with.

Here we are not talking so much about individual mannerisms as about the basic postures that different people adopt as they speak. If someone for example has an involuntary twitch in their left eye it would be both insensitive, and rather silly, to copy it, but if someone has a tendency to sit with their legs crossed, to stroke their chin, or to 'talk with their hands', we should consider mirroring as a conscious way of creating a feeling of empathy. In putting it into practice we must be careful that we do not immediately and obviously jump into every new position that is adopted by the other person. Mirroring is more gradual and subtle and involves displaying the same kind of physical postures if it is to be effective.

We must also, of course, be careful not to spend so much time observing and reflecting these behaviours that we stop listening to what is being said. People who are particularly skilled in this area do it naturally, to the point that it becomes a part of their normal behaviour rather than something that has to be thought about.

Any facilitator who practises this skill will soon learn its power and will want to develop it for use in a wide range of situations. It has the attraction of being both simple to do, with practice, and also very effective. Once, however, I was on a sales visit to an organization and had a meeting with a very 'laid back' training director. At the start of the meeting he sat well back in his chair, I mirrored him. Then he slipped even further back and started combing his hand through his hair. The meeting seemed to be going well so I mirrored that. Then he twisted round in a seemingly impossible position in a tangle of arms and legs, but things were going so well that I decided to try it, and it seemed to work; the discussion was really going well. Then he put his feet up on his desk, observed my look of horror before calmly saying 'I wouldn't advise it if I were you!' We had a good laugh about it, but I didn't sell the job! Despite this, mirroring is a very useful and effective skill to develop, and is well worth practising.

NLP is the study of communication in humans, and it has discovered some remarkable universal traits, a few of which have already been mentioned briefly in the chapter on Understanding Individuals. This is not a detailed text on the subject and anyone interested in following it up in more detail should refer to the list of sources and resources at the back of this book. I recommend that you do, it is fascinating.

One simple skill that is very useful for facilitators stems from the realization that people talk in the way that they think, and that they have a preferred way of thinking which is in one of three modes. Some people think in pictures, others in sounds, and others in feelings. If you watch and listen to people carefully you can pick up the clues that will tell you which one is relevant in the particular situation that you are dealing with currently, and you can mirror this style, which is likely to be much more effective than other styles for that situation. Not doing this is at the bottom of very many of the communication difficulties we all face both at work and at home. Consider this exchange between a married couple:

'I feel upset.'
'Why?'
'I feel that you don't care about me any more.'
'That's nonsense, you know I love you.'
'I feel empty inside.'
'That's completely illogical, I bought you a present just last week.'
'I feel that our relationship has changed.'
'Just explain to me, calmly and simply, what it is that makes you think that.'
'I just feel that it's so.'
'You're impossible!'
'I hate you!'
'I'm going down to the pub!'

Both parties end up aggrieved; they have comprehensively failed to communicate, and it happens all the time. If we analyse the exchange using an elementary knowledge of NLP, it is pretty clear what happened, the second person did not understand the pattern of thinking of the first, and the situation became more and more frustrating for both. It could have been so very different:

'I feel upset.'
'That makes me feel bad too, why is that?'
'I feel that you don't care for me any more.'
'That makes me feel terrible, especially because I love you so much.'
'I feel empty inside.'
'I feel empty as well, when you say that, what can we do?'
'I feel that our relationship has changed.'
'I'm really upset about that especially as I feel the same about you as I always have.'
'Do you really feel the same?'
'I really do.'

Haven't we all been in something like this situation where we failed to talk the same language as the other person and both parties suffered the consequences? It can be avoided if we develop the skills of mirroring the other person's mental thinking pattern through listening to what they say and using the same mode. Of course the example we have just seen is one where the 'customer' is demonstrating clearly that they are in the 'feeling' mode, and therefore we should respond in the same way. Equally it could be that the person we are dealing with says things like, 'The way I view it . . .' or, 'I see us going down this road'. In this example the thinking language is a visual or pictorial one. Or we could be dealing with someone who says things like, 'It sounds to me as if . . .', or 'I'm hearing warning bells ringing here'.

If we as facilitators are aware of the 'inner language' being spoken and if we develop the ability to speak that language normally and naturally, then we have available to us one of the most powerful tools that anyone could wish for to help us to work with other people effectively.

Finally in this chapter on creating empathy there is the issue of vulnerability. As is mentioned in the chapter on Facilitative Behaviours, research indicates that one of the most facilitative of all behaviours is self-disclosure, freely admitting how our own personal experiences match those of the person we are working with. Furthermore self-disclosure is very effective at evoking action on the part of the customer, which is critical to the effectiveness of the facilitator.

Recently I was working with a director of a medium-sized company who had been put into a very different job after a fundamental change of structure in the company. The job was at the same level, if not higher, but it soon became clear that he did not have the skills to perform it well. Quite naturally his competitive instincts made it hard for him to admit this, he blustered on, claiming that all was well, when in fact his performance was going from bad to worse as he actually did less and less. It reached a point where he was doing little more than sitting and hiding in his office all day.

Eventually it was suggested that we met to talk about things. The first hour of the discussion, as I remember it, was all about how the situation was satisfactory, that outside forces were causing any slight problems that there were, and that he would start to do some of the work he knew he should be concentrating on. He was behaving very defensively, that was obvious, yet he seemed also to be wanting help. At the time, I was trying to deal with a personal challenge to do with my health. I was finding it hard to deal with, and it struck me that there was a distinct similarity in our two situations, so I shared it with him. The effect was dramatic. From initial wide-eyed disbelief he progressively felt able to unburden himself of his doubts, his fears and anxieties. He also expressed his determination to succeed. In the months after this session his behaviour changed; he began to do what he said he would; he set himself clear goals for his personal as well as his business development and attacked the challenges with vigour. There was no miraculous transformation in performance, rather a clear and steady improvement which was noted by all around him.

This is an example of the use of self-disclosure as a technique for developing empathy with the express purpose of facilitating and achieving action on the part of the customer. In practice there are two different uses of this mechanism. The first is to reinforce our understanding of a situation that the customer has revealed. In this circumstance we might say something like, 'I can really relate to that because I have had a similar experience . . .'. The result of this intervention is that the customer feels that we do understand the situation and also feels rapport with us.

The second use of the technique is to obtain from the customer his or her own situation by creating an open and sharing atmosphere and a recognition that our and their experience has many similarities so there is nothing to be frightened of or ashamed about. In this case we might say something like, 'I would like to share something with you about myself that I think you may understand . . .'. Here the customer recognizes our willingness to be vulnerable which makes it much easier to be the same. Again this is a powerful way of building empathy and rapport. In both situations using this technique increases the likelihood of action on the part of the customer.

Assessment of skills in building empathy

Think about the following questions carefully, and record your self-evaluation in the spaces provided:

1   Consider your body language. What do you think it tells the people you deal with?

2   Have you ever used body language to elicit a particular response? If not, try it and record what happens.

3   Find some situations where you can use mirroring. Analyse what happens:
     How comfortable did you feel as you were doing it?
     How well did you handle listening while you were mirroring?
     What did you notice about the nature of the interaction?
     How could you improve your skills in mirroring?

4   Listen to yourself as you speak. Based on the words you use what thinking language do you use, visual, auditory or kinesthetic (feelings)?

5   Try to assess the thinking language of the next few people that you meet.
     What were they?
     How easy was it to tell?
     How much harder than normal did you have to concentrate?
     What does this tell you?

6   Practice speaking the same thinking language the next few times you have a discussion with someone. Analyse the experience and establish the learning points for yourself.

7   Find a situation where you can use self-disclosure to create empathy. Analyse the experience:
      How comfortable did you feel?
      How readily did the relevant experience come to mind?
      Did the other person see the relevance of your example?
      How far were you successful in achieving the goal?

8   How good are you at developing empathy with different types of people? Analyse why this is whether you believe yourself to be good or bad.

9   Think of the most empathetic people you know. Take three learning points from your observation of them.

10 Develop an action plan for improving your skills in developing empathy.

11 Listening

Forming the basis of the facilitator role is effective listening, and even more important, hearing. This is easy to say but remains one of the most elusive of skills. It is even more remarkable when we consider how many people believe themselves to be good at listening and are firmly convinced that the problem of communication lies in other people. In practice the vast majority of us are appallingly bad at listening to the words that others are saying, and hearing the meaning that lies behind them.

This is a skill that facilitators must master since their job is to be able to help their customers to progress and develop from where they themselves perceive that they are currently, rather than from where the facilitator thinks or assumes is the starting point. Defining the appropriate course of action requires that the facilitator understands the present position through the eyes of the customer, and clearly this will require an ability to listen.

We have all sat in meetings and watched other people obviously spending their time thinking about what they were going to say next, rather than what the person speaking was talking about, and if we are honest we have all done the same ourselves.

When this occurs a collective monologue is established where, under the guise of a dialogue, what actually is happening is two monologues in parallel with no communication taking place. The following exchange between a production manager and a colleague in marketing illustrates the point:

Marketing: 'Our customers are screaming at us because the deliveries are always late, what are you going to do about it?'

Production: 'The problem with you lot is that you've got no idea how long it takes to do the job properly.'

Marketing: 'If I have to face one more angry customer this week, I think I'll go crazy.'

Production: 'This week alone we've had to cope with 15 per cent absenteeism which makes scheduling a nightmare.'

Marketing: 'What am I supposed to say to someone who insists on a two-week delivery and who threatens me with taking the business away if I don't deliver on time?'

Production: 'Quite apart from the fact that the agreed lead time is four weeks, not two weeks.'

Marketing: 'If I don't meet this schedule I'll lose my bonus as well as a customer.'

Production: 'And the parts are always late in arriving and never in a complete load.'

Marketing: 'I'll just have to contact them, eat humble pie and hope for the best, that's all I can do; I'm surrounded by idiots.'

Production: 'If only other people would do their job properly, I'd be able to do mine, but as it is I'm always the one left carrying the can, it's just unfair.'

Not an ounce of communication has taken place during the whole exchange. Whether at home or in the office or factory the number of situations like this that occur is staggering, and what is worse, for the most part those involved have no idea what is actually happening and merely blame the other party for the failure in understanding.

Facilitators must develop the ability to identify when a collective monologue is happening amongst the people they are dealing with and be able to confront the situation in a positive way and one that does not alienate them. Observations such as:

'Are we sure that we are listening to each other?'

or

'John and Jack, would you like to try and repeat what each of you has just been saying, just so that we can be sure we understand each other's point of view.'

can help in doing this, since they make no direct criticism or judgement that would be likely to breed the negative reaction we would probably elicit if we said:

'The trouble with you two is that you're only interested in your own opinion and you don't listen to what anyone else has to say.'

to which the response from both parties in unison is:

'Yes we do, and what do you know about anything anyway; mind your own business!'

It would be a strategy for bringing the two warring parties together temporarily, but would be successful in achieving little else.

Finally on the subject of collective monologues, we should note that there is an ever-present danger of facilitators themselves falling into the trap. This is most likely to occur as the facilitator is trying to encourage the other person or group to focus on an issue concerning process, while the others involved continue working on the task. Facilitators who find themselves in this situation should 'back off' temporarily, ask themselves why the situation developed like that, and try another route, maybe prefaced with the comment: 'I'd like to make a point about the process that I think is affecting our work, so can we stop working on the task for a moment, is that OK?'

The problem of selective perception is another issue that affects our ability to listen and hear. Again something that is very common, selective perception has no place in the facilitator role because it is indicative of a closed mind and of not being prepared to start from where the other person is. Even if we can manage the tendency in ourselves, this is something that we will come across time and time again in those that we are working with.

Selective perception is the tendency in all of us to interpret what we hear purely in our own terms and to reject or simply omit information that does not fit with what we either expected or wanted to hear or see. Since this happens largely at the subconscious level, it is something that people do not tend to recognize in themselves, so the facilitator has a particularly important job in spotting it when it occurs, and in confronting it with sensitivity. Again, observations that can help include:

'Can we just check that we understand the full implications of what's just been said.'
'I'd just like to check that I really heard what John has said. My understanding was that . . . , which would mean that . . . Is that the way that you see it, Sally?'

Concentration is one of the main keys to listening. Consider the following exchange:

Person A	'Is this Wembley?'
Person B	'No, it's Thursday.'
Person A	'So am I, let's go for a drink!'

To be blunt, listening is plain hard work, which is maybe why so many of us are so bad at it! If we are concentrating on what the other person is saying there is no room for us to be making assumptions about the meaning that lies behind the words, and if this is not clear we should ask for clarification. This sounds obvious, but strangely many people find it remarkably difficult to do, presumably because in some way we associate it with an admission of 'guilt' which is maybe for many of us a throwback to our early childhood and schooldays when we may have been punished for not paying attention.

'Could you say that again please?'
'Could you repeat that in a different way so I can be sure I understand?'
'Sorry, I just didn't hear that.'

These are all simple ways of asking for clarification, that cause neither pain nor loss of face. If facilitators find that they are not using them, it is likely that they are relying on their assumptions and guesses rather than an understanding of the other person, since no one in this role can permanently sustain the level of concentration that is truly required. Our purpose is to understand what is being said from the other person's point of view, which must be our starting point if we are to assist in the development process, and we must be prepared to do whatever is necessary to ensure that this happens.

If we are to be good at hearing the true meaning that lies behind the words we also need to develop our skills in checking out that we have really heard what the other person was trying to say. This is important since it is so easy to misinterpret words and their nuances and also because we tend to relate what we hear to our own experience and to make assumptions on that basis. This is probably the biggest trap in the whole field of communication, and the one that we all fall into most often.

Since, as facilitators, we are interested, exclusively, in understanding and building on the situation as it is perceived by our customer, we must be sure that we are diagnosing it accurately. The skill here is to reflect back in our own words the sense and meaning that we have taken from our customer's statement, and this is done by prefacing our response with the words, 'what I heard you say was . . .'.

When we have finished we need to be sure that we listen to any further observation and that we do not become defensive about any misinterpretation on our part. It will do us no good if, having got it wrong, we say 'but you didn't say that'. The process of reflecting back is designed for us to clarify and be sure of our understanding, not to prove what good listeners we are. The exercise also has the great strength that it gives the other person the chance to review his or her statement and to check that it was what was meant.

In some ways the facilitator's job is similar to that of a detective, piecing together fragments of information and evidence in an attempt to build a full picture of the situation. As facilitators we are interested in helping our customers to commit themselves to action plans that will help them and their organizations, but often it is not immediately clear to anyone what should be done. A useful tool that helps to 'tease out' possibilities for improvement is for us to listen for clues in what the customer is saying. This technique is also very powerful in generating commitment to action.

Very often as they are talking, people indicate areas of their performance that they believe can be improved, or that they wish they could accomplish better, but these potential action points are often lost in the overall flow of the discussion. This technique involves our listening carefully to what the customer is saying, specifically for any expressions of concern about an issue or interest in a subject. These subjects all represent potential action areas for the customer, but often they need picking up and developing before an action plan can be formed. In the normal course of events most of these clues go unnoticed and so opportunity for improvement is lost. In following up these clues the facilitator first of all should verify the level of concern or interest and the potential benefit to be derived from an improvement activity based on the particular area. Though every improvement, however apparently insignificant, is to be valued, there is the legitimate issue of prioritizing to be taken into account. If a subject is deemed too minor to deal with at the moment, it should be noted by the facilitator and brought up at a later date. Certainly only the one or two more important or pressing issues should be developed at any time since we do not want to overburden our customers with too many issues all at the same time, since this is likely to be very demotivating.

In listening for clues we are trying to identify areas of interest or concern. These are likely to be expressed in terms such as, 'I was worried when . . .', 'I thought I could have done better when . . .', 'I wish . . .', 'If only . . .' and so on. When facilitators hear such expressions from the leaders that they are working with they should concentrate immediately on trying to understand the clue and working out how to explore it further and translate it into an effective action commitment. This can be done by asking questions such as 'What do you think you should do about that?' or 'How can you turn that concern into a positive improvement goal?' Using the power of NLP, questions can, of course be phrased in the most suitable language for the particular person we are dealing with, for example, if the customer is 'visual', we could say, 'What do you see yourself doing about that?', if 'audio' we could say 'I hear what you say, if you could turn that concern into a positive action point, you could make music with it!', or if a 'feelings' person we could say 'What do you feel you should do about this issue?'

In developing 'clues' and helping people turn them into positive action points we should always be conscious of the need to record the commitment, and since they are our customers' action points, they should write them down. Trivial though this might seem it is important as a mechanism for increasing the level of ownership that is felt for the improvement activity concerned.

In groups a frequent barrier to listening, hearing and understanding is 'multi-speak'. This describes the situation in groups when more than one person is speaking at the same time. When this occurs listening and hearing stop, because it is impossible to concentrate on what more than one person is saying at any one time. Though groups tend to deny that this happens in their meetings, in fact it happens all the time. The fact that many people do not recognize it probably indicates that they were only interested in what they were saying, rather than the contributions of others that were being made at the same time. Because facilitators are interested in hearing what each member of the group has to say, and in trying to make it possible for every group member to do the same, this is something that we need to be able to deal with quickly and effectively, for example by comments such as:

'Can we just have one person at a time please?'
'Hang on, you first Jane.'
'Sorry, I want to understand what both of you are saying, you first Jim.'

It is so simple and yet so often 'multi-speak' goes on and on. In fact the longer it goes on it seems, the less people recognize it and the more the meeting will tend to fragment into subgroups carrying on their own conversation regardless. This happens in groups at all levels of organizations, and facilitators will find themselves constantly having to intervene to pull the discussion back into one that everyone, including the facilitator, can have a chance of hearing and understanding.

Listening questionnaire

Answer the following questions, relating to listening, honestly and write down your responses:

1   Think of three occasions in the past week when you have not listened to what someone else was saying carefully enough to be sure you really understood. Write them down together with your assessment of the worst possible consequences. Note that if you cannot think of any examples, you are either not being honest with yourself, or you are not yet analysing and evaluating your behaviour accurately.

2   What is the most important barrier to accurate listening in your character?

3   Who is the best listener you know?

4   What is it about this person that makes him or her good at listening?

5   What is it about you that makes you not as good as this person?

6   Assess your performance in listening for and developing clues.

7   What two or three actions do you intend to take that will help you to improve your listening skills?

8   How will you obtain feedback about and measure your improvement?

12 Eliciting

For the facilitator to be able to hear what is being said, there is an obvious need to elicit contributions in the first place. This is another key skill area and is by no means as straightforward and easy as at first it seems. So what skills does the facilitator need to develop in this area?

First there is the ability to ask open questions, and to do this normally and naturally. People are taught on training courses the value of open questions, but few ever put the learning to any use. Asking open questions is fundamental to the role because it is crucial to establishing where the customer is coming from and where he or she wants to get to. Open questions are those that cannot be answered with a straight 'yes' or 'no', but require further elaboration. These questions start with words such as what, where, why, when, who and how. Sometimes it is difficult to frame a question like this so that it sounds natural, so another very useful phrase for the start of a question is 'to what extent...', so for example rather than saying 'do you like work?' which draws a yes or no response, we could ask 'to what extent do you like work?' which is likely to give the facilitator more to build on.

It is surprising how often people believe that they are asking open questions when in fact they are not, and this applies to facilitators as well as everyone else, so it is important to be conscious of the issue. If we find ourselves asking many questions it is quite likely that we are asking closed ones, or at least ones that were not of a high enough quality to elicit a full response, especially from someone who is reticent for one reason or another. For example the open question given above: 'To what extent do you like work?' could be answered, 'I don't' by someone like this. In a situation such as this the facilitator needs to follow on with more open questions in an attempt to open up the issue that is being explored at the time. This can be done with questions such as:

'Oh, that's interesting, why is that?'
'What do you think is the reason for that?'

or, if these do not work, with:

'Really? That's interesting, I would have thought that you . . .'

which is more of an open 'non-question', but which often helps to facilitate a more open and flowing discussion.

The second skill needed in the area of eliciting lies in managing and using our non-verbal communication to positive effect. Over 80 per cent of all communication is non-verbal and so if facilitators are not actively working in this area they are seriously limiting their potential effectiveness. There are a number of very useful skills that can be used here, such as building in regular non-verbal approbation while the other person is speaking. Nodding is the obvious example of this and others include leaning forward, which gives a non-verbal message of interest, and smiling positively. Would-be facilitators should experiment and practise in this area, however silly or awkward this might seem, since it is so important. Hold a discussion where you offer the absolute minimum of non-verbal feedback, be as deadpan as possible and see what happens: compare this to the response you get when you actively manage this dimension of your behaviour, and here experiment with sending negative as well as positive non-verbal messages, for example by frowning, sitting back in your chair and looking bored, shaking your head and so on. You will not want to do this while working with real customers, but it is something that can be done, for example, with other facilitators, selected friends or, for the brave, the family!

The active use of silence is another key skill in this category. Most people find silence acutely embarrassing and will 'fill the space' when a silence occurs. This is sometimes done by using ritual expressions like 'very interesting' which usually means 'I'm bored stiff' when used in this way! Alternatively people fill space with their own answers to the question, their own views, beliefs or opinions; anything to stop the silence. From the facilitator's point of view this is damaging since we are trying to encourage the customer to think something through. If we want sensible answers we must allow time, where necessary, for consideration.

It is perfectly natural to find silence awkward and so it is useful to have a way of building it into our approach. In practice people fill gaps in conversations or discussions very quickly. A silence of two seconds very often seems like an eternity, and three or four seconds can become excruciatingly embarrassing. The facilitator though wants considered, not ritual, answers to the questions posed and so must allow time for consideration. One way to manage our inclination to jump in and fill the silence is to try counting to ten, slowly. This gives ten second's worth of thinking time for the person we are working with. Counting to ten in this way gives us something to do and helps prevent our breaking in to this valuable time. Of course we should be actively managing our body language as we are doing this; looking expectant, but also relaxed, positive and encouraging.

Occasionally we meet people who find it genuinely difficult to think of anything to say after having been asked a question, and so we need to be on the lookout for this, since we do not want them to feel that they are being pressurized or exposed. Of course there is a danger that we are responding to our own needs to have the silence ended, but assuming that we can control this, if the silence is going on too long, we might say, 'what do you

think?' to avoid discomfort and to give additional encouragement. In this situation, sometimes, the question has been forgot-
ten or lost in a parallel thought process and so we should be
prepared to repeat it if necessary.

Finally, on rare occasions we may come across someone who
plays games with silence. Many years ago I was running a training course for a group of sales staff from an insurance company.
There were about 15 of them on the programme, and to be honest
they were treating the whole event in a rather cavalier fashion.

At one point I asked a question that I thought was particularly
pertinent and thought-provoking. There was a silence that I
interpreted as thinking time, and I remember being quite
pleased with myself. The silence went on for quite a while but I
went along with it. It continued and I began to feel distinctly
uncomfortable as I looked at 15 faces looking at me. In the end,
after what seemed like an eternity I said, 'well what do you
think?', at which point all 15 of them simultaneously collapsed in
fits of laughter, and a chorus of, 'We won! We won!' The fact that
I remember the occasion so vividly after so many years gives an
indication of the intensity of my feelings at the time!

The fact that eliciting information from those that we are
working with is a key part of the facilitator role should not be
taken to mean that all we do is ask questions and wait for an
answer. We also have legitimate and important information and
views that can help our customers. Because of this the subject of
managing the 'talking ratio' is something that we need to take
into account as a part of this subject. The talking ratio is simply
the amount of time in any discussion that each party is talking.

For the reasons that have been discussed already there is a tendency for the balance to be weighted to the facilitator unless it is
managed otherwise. Typically new or untrained facilitators con-
sume over 70 per cent of the discussions they have with their
customers as they 'tell' their customer their version of reality,
and then try to 'sell' this view. Where this is the case it is the facilitator's view that is being used, often to the exclusion of that of
the other party, and clearly this is not the purpose of the meeting,
neither is it likely to be effective.

Studies have shown that where the facilitator does less than 40 per cent of the talking a number of important outcomes tend to result:

1 There is a greater likelihood of constructive action, especially when the other party is fully involved in setting goals, priorities and targets.
2 It is less likely that there will be arguments about what should be done.
3 The other party will feel more motivated to action.
4 It is more likely that the other party will be able to diagnose his or her own problems.
5 The facilitator will learn more about the other person, and this knowledge will lead to a more positive assessment of the other person's performance.

Since facilitators are concerned with helping people to improve and with developing self-sufficiency in this process, the first, third and fourth of these outcomes are especially important, so being able to manage the talking ratio to something like this 40/60 split is a very relevant skill as we start working with someone. As our relationship develops, and as people demonstrate, mainly to themselves, that they can diagnose and prioritize their problems and improvement opportunities, the talking ratio can be managed to allow even more time for the other person, until ultimately, with the ratio at 0/100, the facilitator can withdraw safe in the knowledge that the ability and willingness to continue working on improvement is in place.

At the outset the 40 per cent of the discussion that can be filled by the facilitator of course has to be handled carefully, using the skills that are dealt with in this chapter. Specifically we will want to give our feedback in a way that makes it likely that it will be heard, understood and used. With this in mind it is a good general rule that we should share with our customer our perceptions, recognizing that they are indeed perceptions, not statements of objective truth.

What we are doing is to offer an alternative way of viewing the situation that will help to aid clarity. If we are navigating and wish to plot a course to a particular destination, we will need at least two points of which we are certain to be able to calculate our route accurately. In providing our customers with our view we are offering an additional point of reference that can be used, together with their own, as the inputs required to plot the desired course of action. Since any individual's 'picture of reality' is probably somewhat distorted, having two views available can help to accommodate and correct this, and achieve a more accurate picture on which to base decisions.

Diagnosis of skills in eliciting information

Think carefully about the following questions and record your self-diagnosis in the spaces provided:

1   How good do you believe you are in the use of open questions? What evidence do you have for your opinion?

2   What open questions do you use routinely?

3   How do you manage yourself to use silence effectively? What difficulties do you face in doing this, and how do you handle them?

4   Typically what is the talking ratio in your discussions with other individuals? When was the last time you consciously planned a particular talking ratio prior to a discussion, what was it and what happened?

5　How will you obtain accurate feedback about the actual talking ratio in a series of discussions, so that you can manage it more effectively?

6　Who in your experience has been most successful in eliciting information from you? What can you learn from this?

7　Develop a set of goals to help you improve your skills in eliciting information. Try to build in measures that will give you feedback.

13 Positive confrontation

The facilitator role is not a passive one, merely reflecting and agreeing with anything that the customer says, it is much more positive and active than this. The fact is that most people do not think in a straightforward manner, especially when they are embarking on a journey into the unknown, so the role of the facilitator is to help people to isolate and address issues more simply than they would otherwise do, and to arrive at sensible decisions that they are committed to and will action. It is not that the ability to think in an uncomplicated way is beyond people, merely that the territory is new and that assistance is often needed to achieve the clarity that is required if the resulting action is to be productive.

The facilitator must be able to highlight muddled, dishonest or inappropriate thinking and to confront it, but to do so in a way that does not provoke defensiveness or a loss of ownership. It is, then, an active role, and one requiring much skill, since there is an ever-present danger of provoking defensive reactions that will do nothing to help the situation, and will in practice probably deflect the discussion away from where it should be.

Some of the most difficult situations that facilitators have to deal with are those where we have an input to make which is at variance from the views held by those that we are working with. This is because most people's perceptions of themselves and evaluation of other information about them has been the subject of rationalization. Put simply, we are likely to reject data that does not fit our preferred preconception, especially if it is expressed in a way that makes it easy for this to happen. How often do we hear, and indeed say ourselves, 'yes, but you don't understand the full situation', 'yes, but I only did it because . . .', and 'yes, but they did it first'?

Unless as facilitators we are able to deal successfully with giving information or feedback that is contrary to the perception of our customers it is hard to see that we can be effective. Indeed all we would end up doing would be to repeat what they said and add nothing. This is easy to say, but the question is, how do we handle this delicate area?

One of the main causes of ineffectiveness in relationships is the tendency that most people have to judge the other person's opinion or contribution in terms of black or white. Responses such as 'you are wrong', 'that is rubbish', or 'you don't understand the situation' are examples of this type of reaction. The problem with this approach, which is justified by those who use it as being honest and straightforward, is that it does not work, because all that it does is to elicit defensive reactions and a win/lose atmosphere. It is very unlikely that the object of the feedback will accept what has been said: it is much more likely that it will draw out a 'yes, but . . .' response, and then be ignored. At worst it will also do irreparable damage to any feelings of empathy and rapport, and so will render the facilitator entirely ineffective.

So what are facilitators to do when they either do not agree or believe that something is wrong with, or missing from, the statement that has been made? Many people, if they do not want to risk the reaction that is likely from making direct judgements, will avoid saying anything at all, which is, of course, just as inappropriate, although often quite tempting. What is required is a way of putting our view without running the risk of this kind of negative response, and so the answer here is in what is technically known as non-evaluative, descriptive feedback, or to use less jargon, in describing not judging. Since the only reality lies in the perceptions that people have, there are no objective rights or wrongs, certainly in the sort of issues that are likely to be the subject of such discussions.

It is crucial for us to understand this, but also to have available a way of sharing our perceptions that contributes to, rather than detracts from, the discussion. The key phrases here are ones such as 'I feel', 'the way I see it' or 'I believe'. These are much less directly confrontational than 'You are' or 'You aren't' or any other judgemental statement, and yet they do share an alternative perception, and so give the customer the opportunity of rethinking, which is unlikely if a defensive, win/lose situation has been created.

We are often so judgemental, that considerable practice is usually needed to get into the habit of phrasing our feedback in this way, but it is well worth it. Do not think, either, that all this amounts to is being wishy-washy and mealy-mouthed. In fact, because this way of responding causes further thought and cannot simply be rationalized away, it is much tougher in practice than so-called 'tough', judgemental feedback.

We tend not to think about giving feedback in this way and so it is a skill that we can all usefully practise. This will involve setting ourselves goals for giving descriptive feedback, and setting some criteria for evaluation of the results that are achieved. One person who did this was a senior manager who had set himself the objective of confronting the inconsistent behaviour that he observed in his managing director specifically, and in the rest of the senior team in general. He could see how to confront his colleagues because they presented less of a threat, but was unsure of how to give feedback to his boss. It became clear in discussion that his strategy was actually highly judgmental; he was just going to tell them what they were doing wrong.

When he thought through this plan he was the first to admit that it probably would not work, and that all it was likely to achieve was to make him feel better in the short term. Having grasped the idea of descriptive rather than evaluative feedback, he was able to see conceptually how this would enable him to give feedback to anyone, regardless of their reporting relation-ship. He was, however, unsure of precisely what to say and how to say it, but it did not take long for him to develop a series of phrases that he felt comfortable in using. He developed targets for himself in using these phrases, and over a period of four weeks practised his new-found skill.

He was not only surprised at the results when he used them, but was equally surprised at the difference in reaction that he observed when he either forgot, and lapsed into judgemental feedback, or used the phrases awkwardly. He reported that both his boss and his colleagues seemed much less defensive about what he had to say, his inputs were used rather than being rejected as had often been the case in the past, and occasionally, to his amazement, he was thanked for putting forward useful views!

Whereas confronting issues in this way will be successful on most occasions, it has to be said that there are times when it will appear not to work so well. This usually happens when people have such a fixed view, and are so intent on it that they simply do not hear the precise words that are being spoken, they interpret descriptive feedback as judgemental, and so reject it. In these cir-cumstances we must not lapse back into the evaluative mode since this will certainly not help. In practice what is necessary here is to be even more descriptive, but first we should check whether we are using precisely the right words and are matching the 'thinking language' of the other person. Provided that we are, it is often an effective way of getting people at least to hear alternative feedback to preface it with, 'I may not be right in this but I feel that/the way I see it/it sounds to me like ... is worth thinking about' and then to conclude with, 'Accepting that we should always take into account more than one interpretation, what do you think are the aspects of this view that you could use successfully?'

If this intervention does not work as far as encouraging the other person to listen to alternative views and interpretations, the next step involves reinforcing the fact that people believe their own perceptions, and making the point that, whether these alternative views are correct or not is not the issue; the point is that we have to live with the consequences of the perceptions that others have, and that we disregard them at our peril, since very often they have an influence on our own effectiveness. We should go on to suggest that it will be better to try to understand different views, whether we agree with them or not, simply on the basis that we are concerned to optimize our own performance. There is an ideal opportunity here for self-disclosure, giving an example if there is one available from our own experience, that shows how dangerous it is to ignore or reject alternative views.

Positive confrontation questionnaire

Think carefully about the following questions, answer them honestly and in writing in the spaces provided:

1   How judgemental do you tend to be in the way that you normally give feedback?

2   Think of two or three examples of when you have been judgemental in giving feedback. What reactions have you had? Be precise, analyse the responses you got carefully.

3   To what extent do you tend to avoid giving feedback when you perceive that there is a danger that it will cause conflict and be rejected?

4   Overall, to what extent are you a 'judger' or an 'avoider'?

5   What useful non-evaluative phrases would you be comfortable using in sharing information that does not match the perception of your customer?

6   What are the two or three issues that you would most like to confront with other people, but have avoided until now?

7   Construct scenarios where you use descriptive feedback as a way of confronting these issues. Write down how the discussion might go and how you could respond to different eventualities.

8   Develop an action plan for improving your performance in positive confrontation.

14   The Emperor's new clothes

One factor that most inhibits improvement is the difficulty that most people have when it comes to giving 'negative' feedback. This happens all the time and occurs especially when the feedback involves someone more senior in the organizational hierarchy. We have all heard the story of 'the Emperor's new clothes', where the Emperor was sold a new set of 'clothes', which were not clothes at all, in fact he was naked. The 'confidence trick' was made powerful by the announcement that the clothes were very beautiful, but that a fool would not be able to see them. It took a child to reveal the truth.

The story is of great relevance to facilitators since organizations are full of people who have views about others, indeed who express them privately, but are not prepared to tell the person concerned. In one organization, as an example, the engineering director was the subject of considerable criticism from his colleagues. They talked about him and his inadequacies endlessly amongst themselves; they said that he did not do as he said he would, that he held up work by taking too long, that he was defensive and a block to progress; they cited example after example to each other, but not to him.

The person concerned, not having been told anything different, thought that he was doing a good job under difficult circumstances, since he claimed that the other directors did not specify what they needed clearly enough. He was not prepared to accept the feedback, which was the views of the other directors, when I gave it to him, so we agreed a process which involved his asking his colleagues. He came back and said that he had done so and that everyone had said that everything was all right!

In another organization the managing director was the subject of much criticism, again privately, among his colleagues. When I asked the directors what he had said when they had given him the feedback that they were now giving me, they said, in effect that I must be joking if I thought that they were going to tell him; that they had families and mortgages and that they wanted to keep their jobs! When I suggested that if he was causing that much mayhem that the company would not survive and they would lose their jobs anyway, their response was that this was why I was there, and that it was my job to tell him! In their terms, presumably, I was expendable!

These are particular examples of situations that are repeated endlessly in organizations everywhere. For facilitators they are important not only because they need to be confronted but also because it is likely that, in the absence of an outside consultant, the facilitator will be expected to deal with them.

There is no doubt that these are difficult situations to handle. Anyone would be justifiably concerned about giving feedback if their experience tells them that they will be putting themselves at risk by giving it. There is a remarkable tendency amongst people to 'shoot the messenger', or at least for us to assume that the messenger will be shot. I have lost count of the number of times senior people in organizations have said to me, 'Mike, I want you to be completely open and honest with me. If there is anything that I should know about myself, I want you to tell me however negative it is.' Equally I have lost count of the times that I have bitten that bullet, given some feedback, and immediately had my kneecaps shot off! 'That's rubbish', 'who told you that?', 'you don't understand the situation', 'give me specific examples (for me to use in refuting the accusation)', 'what?'. These are typical responses, and all delivered in a tone of voice that indicated to me that I had better watch my tongue. It is fascinating as well how often, when I have agreed with something that they have said or done, that such people will say, while preening themselves, 'you mustn't just agree with me, Mike, you have to tell me where I am going wrong'!

What is happening here is that a game is being set up, very much like 'the Emperor's new clothes': many people will say that they want to hear 'the truth' but in fact that is the last thing they are prepared for, unless it reinforces what they want to hear. Many people make it extremely difficult to give feedback to them in anything like a direct way; they react both defensively and aggressively. People learn very quickly where this is the case, and will studiously avoid giving any negative feedback; thus the 'Emperor' continues with the self-delusion, and everybody else continues to talk about it in private.

Obviously this is not a recipe for success, and since facilitators are concerned with the improvement of their organizations they will need to be both able and willing to deal with such situations using whatever means are necessary. If direct approaches do not work, then facilitators need to work in more subtle ways; what they must not do is to fall into the same trap as others and to avoid the issue.

The difficulty of dealing with this phenomenon as facilitators is that we are faced with a number of powerful human traits at the same time. First, 'Emperors' tend to have a very well-developed self-image and would do almost anything to protect it. They usually interpret feedback in terms of strength and weakness, and they want to see themselves, and for others to see them, as strong. Second, they are usually very competitive and they see life as a competition which they intend to win. Third, though they appear to be outgoing and confident, underneath they are just as unsure as the rest of us, but they believe that they cannot afford to let this show because it might damage the self-image that they have cultivated over the years. This often shows itself in high levels of defensive aggression when threatened. In the normal run of events, however, they will actively request feedback on the assumption that it will reinforce their self-image. Next they tend to have an even greater ability to rational-ize their own behaviour than those around them, which has the effect of forming what at times appears to be an almost impene-trable web of self-delusion. Finally they tend to be very judge-mental, interpreting what they see around them as good or bad, right or wrong, and they have unquestioning faith in their belief that they are both good and right.

At first glance this does not paint a particularly pleasant pic-ture, but it needs to be said that such people are very often pleas-ant and charming in their routine dealings with others. They will often see themselves as 'people people', and they would, with-out exception, be mortified if they knew that the above descrip-tion applied to them! It is also worth saying that they are often very successful in their careers, which is fine, but it makes the phenomenon even more difficult to deal with for us as facilita-tors.

The key to understanding and dealing with Emperors is that it is very difficult to confront them 'head on', especially if they are in a more senior position than we are, so more subtle approaches are needed that do not immediately threaten their self-image, and yet achieve the objective, which in one way or another involves a commitment to action designed to improve their per-formance, either by stopping doing something that is impeding progress, or by setting goals for the development of new and more productive behaviours.

The tactics for dealing with Emperors will be different depending on whether the person concerned is the most senior manager or whether there is an immediate peer group that can be utilized. In most circumstances the second of these situations is rather easier to deal with, but they both need care and skill if the facilitator is to succeed.

Where there is a peer group, probably the best approach is to build on the Emperor's need for approbation. This can be achieved in one of two ways, whichever fits the particular cir-cumstance. The first possibility is to talk in terms of the need of the peer group for a real and visible role model of the improve-ment process, and to position the Emperor as the ideal candidate for this given the high esteem in which he or she is held.

An important part of this strategy is to make the point that though in a sense it does not matter what issue is chosen to work on, it makes sense for it to be something that will be worth while, both for the person concerned and also others in the organization that could benefit, either as customers or suppliers. With this idea in place the facilitator can play a part in helping to make the decision about the subject of the improvement effort safe in the knowledge that any defensiveness can be countered with a reminder that the underlying purpose of the plan is to demonstrate a role model of the improvement process.

The second possibility is to share the feedback which the peer group has avoided giving, and this time to make the point that perceptions are strange things, and to stress the importance of not becoming defensive about it, 'rising above it' in effect. Having done this the next step is to explain how people who are very successful are able to succeed in other people's terms as well as their own, and that therefore there is an opportunity within the feedback to set some goals that will make this the case with the particular peer group in question.

Where the Emperor is the senior manager the approach needs to be somewhat different, although based on the same underlying philosophy. In this situation it never does any harm to begin by reinforcing our appreciation of the complexity and the 'loneliness' of the top position, and making the point that few people fully understand this. Next it is worth talking about the difficulty, at this level of the organization, of finding improvement possibilities that are visible enough to provide a clear example to the organization as a whole, but to reinforce the importance of doing this since people in organizations invariably follow the behavioural lead given them by their leader. At this point ideas can be generated that could fulfil the requirement, including some added in by the facilitator. Once the relevant issue has been identified and the plans made, the facilitator should remember to reinforce the point that the real importance of achieving success in the plan is to provide a clear message, and encouragement, to everyone else in the organization.

In both of these situations the key for the facilitator lies in displacing the need for the improvement away from the person concerned and on to someone or something else. This is always an appealing idea for Emperors and can be made even more powerful if it can be demonstrated that the main benefits will be felt by these other people. When working with people such as this the facilitator must have developed excellent rapport and must demonstrate genuine interest and concern for this particular person in this particular situation. The ability to demonstrate empathy is also a very important part of the process. Without these ingredients the approach is unlikely to succeed.

15 'Facipulation'

Facilitation, as it is described and discussed in this book concerns helping people to come to a view about what they believe they should do in the cause of improvement, whether working individually or in groups. Facilitation does not involve manipulating them into an acceptance of a course of action that has been predetermined by someone else.

Though the whole process of 'pure' facilitation is very powerful, and works very successfully in most cases, it has to be said that there are occasions when it does not. There are instances where those that we are dealing with are intractable and are not prepared to work on improvement, or they refuse to see issues in any way other than their own and will not work with a third party. Though rare, such instances do occur from time to time, and there is little that can be done about them.

It also happens occasionally that the people we are working with, either individually or in groups, fail to see an obvious opportunity or course of action. In cases such as these there is sometimes a case for the facilitator straying into the task area if it can be done in an appropriate way and if it leaves the ownership

of the agreed action genuinely with the person or people concerned. We have coined a term for this kind of intervention and
we call it 'facipulation'. It should be stressed that though an
important weapon in the facilitator's armoury, it should be handled with great care, and should most definitely not be used as
an excuse for the facilitator to become involved in the 'action' of
working on the task at the expense of concentrating on the
process.

We should all recognize as well that there is nothing extra
clever in using facipulation, it is in many ways a last resort when
we have not succeeded through the use of pure facilitation. To
save ourselves from the feeling that we are being clever when we
use it, we should all perhaps reflect on the fact that, had we been
better facilitators, we would not have needed to go down this
path. The following cases are given in this spirit.

An example of 'facipulation' at an individual level concerns
the managing director of an organization that we were assisting
with the introduction of a Total Quality process. The person
involved was a very dynamic and powerful man who did not
suffer fools gladly. He had told me that he hated indirectness and
dishonesty and that I was to be open and straight with him concerning everything, including feedback about himself. Everyone
else in the organization told me that it was impossible to give
him any feedback about himself because of his aggressive and
negative response whenever anyone had tried, which they had
all stopped doing! I felt very vulnerable.

The fact was that his behaviour was impeding improvement
in the organization because people saw the demand for it as a
case of 'do as I say, not as I do', and they were not prepared to put
their energy behind a process that seemed to them to be 'unfair'.
This was especially so because it was their perception that he
was the one who caused most of the problems, first because of
his aggressive attitude, and second because he constantly inter-
rupted people's work with impromptu, crisis meetings, he was
often late for meetings that had been planned, and sometimes
did not turn up at all because something had happened that
needed his urgent attention. For his part, I think genuinely, he
did not see this.

In one of my meetings with him I broached the subject of the need for him to have a plan for working on his own improvement. I did this in the context of other people in the organization needing to see a role model of personal improvement actually happening if they were to be able to understand what was needed, and not to be defensive about the apparent admission of weakness that personal improvement is often seen to imply. In effect then, I was deflecting the need somewhat away from him improving because he needed to, on to the need for him to help others in his organization through his example. He bridled a bit to start with, then accepted the point intellectually, but said that he could not think of anything that would serve the purpose, and asked if I had any ideas.

As has been said in the chapter on 'the Emperor's new clothes', this question is often a trap, and was certainly one that I wanted to avoid, so I asked him to think of anything that he did that would be visible to the organization if he changed and improved it. He said he could not think of anything, and asked me again for a suggestion. I said that the issue need not be a very big one, but that it had to be visible since one of the reasons for doing it was to be able to demonstrate the process of personal improvement to the organization. Again he said he could not think of anything, and again he asked me for suggestions.

At this point I summarized the requirement and the reasoning that led to it and reinforced the point that the main requirement was to do something that was visible. I then said that since he spent much of his time with other people in meetings, time management was an obvious possibility, and asked him how he felt about his management of time. After we had gone through all the reasons why it was difficult, in a job like his, to manage time well, we agreed that this was a visible issue, and one that, if he could improve in it, would send a clear message to the whole organization, so it was an appropriate one to achieve the objective. He committed himself to managing his time better, bought himself an electronic diary, used it and became a role model to us all. Tangentially the benefit to the organization was a huge reduction in wasted time.

An example of 'facipulation' while involved in working with a group comes from a task force of engineers who were looking at a problem of congestion in their workshop. The group had, as many do, started their work on the assumption that they already had the answer, which was to build them a bigger place in which to work. They believed that they had solved the problem, but had been persuaded, not very willingly, to go through a rigorous problem-solving process rather than simply to accept this possible solution without any proper analysis.

They collected data and analysed it, and began to look for solutions. At this stage they again began to go back to the issue of a new workshop. The more they talked about it the more they persuaded themselves that it was not only a good idea, but the only idea. It was a classic example of 'groupthink' as described in Chapter 3. Even when they were persuaded to undertake a cost-benefit analysis of this solution and found out just how expensive it would be, they managed to persuade themselves that it would be a test of management interest and commitment whether or not they accepted the group's recommendation.

Frankly it was obvious that the idea was completely 'unsaleable' to management. Not only was the cost prohibitive, there was also a serious issue about where such a workshop could be placed, and what is more there were a number of other options that, at face value, seemed to offer more potential. In this particular situation however the group was in no mood to listen to this kind of reasoning; they had convinced themselves apart from anything else about this test of management commitment.

In these circumstances the facilitator decided to build on their belief, so it was suggested to them that, as a part of their presentation to management, and to demonstrate how thoroughly they had done their job, they should be able to present a couple of options that they had rejected along with the relevant arguments and the cost-benefit analyses.

The group accepted this, albeit a little grudgingly, but asked what other possible solutions there were. One or two were suggested including the purchase of a racking system for the storage of the tools and equipment that were causing the congestion. They did some work on investigating racking systems, and began to realize that this was a much less expensive option that would still solve their problem. Some of the group, however, kept pressing for the original proposal until it was pointed out that the group, if it accepted the racking solution, would be able to demonstrate in its presentation and recommendations not only its ability to solve the problem, but also the fact that they were concerned enough about the company having to spend money for them to rethink their original proposal, and that there was, therefore, a double benefit in this case which was bound to bring additional recognition while still involving management in demonstrating commitment through the purchase of the new racking.

In both of the examples that have been given the person or group involved needed to feel a clear sense of ownership of the course of action that was agreed, and this will always be so. In cases such as these, of course, purists could level the accusation of having strayed into the area of task, and could point out that this is not the preserve of the facilitator. My answer is that there are occasions when this kind of intervention is both justifiable and necessary, though I accept that they need to be handled with great caution, and that they must not be used as an excuse on the part of facilitators to get involved in the task and to show how clever they are; as was said earlier if we have to resort to 'facipulation', it merely indicates that we were not skilled enough in using the normal tools of our trade.

PART IV
The Facilitator Role in Practice

The role of facilitator is a down-to-earth and practical one although being firmly based on solid and well-understood theories about organizations, groups and individuals. Unless the practising exponent is able to demonstrate tangible worth there will be little sympathy for the role and it will not be used.

There is an increasing range of situations where facilitators are being utilized, and very successfully too; though it is worth saying that the more complex the circumstances where the facilitator is used, the more necessary it is for the person to have been trained in advanced skills. Working with a problem-solving group consisting of junior staff is one thing; working with a board of directors can be quite another. Equally working with individuals also requires a set of skills that many existing facilitators have not, as yet, been equipped with.

In Part IV we look at some of the basic issues that need to concern the facilitator as well as a range of different situations in which facilitators are now being used to assist. Next we gain an insight into the role in practice by considering some real-life cases from different organizations, and analysing the facilitator's performance. Finally, structures are recommended for approaching the main contexts that the facilitator will work in.

16 Issues for the facilitator

There are a number of general issues that any facilitator must take into account and involve understanding and skill if they are not to impede progress. Introducing a facilitator either to an individual or a group is still an unusual event in most organizations and for most people, so it needs to be handled with care.

It is quite probable that the initial response from the customer will be defensive since the inference likely to be drawn is that someone has been brought in because there is some doubt about the ability of the person or people to do the job, or to handle the situation that is presented. Because of this there is a need for a carefully thought through synopsis of the purpose of the facilitator role and a clear statement that it does not imply any unusual inadequacy, but that it is an entirely positive approach based on the desire to ensure that both the person and the organization achieve the best result from the opportunity for improvement. It is also worth stressing the point that the use of facilitators is, or will be in the future, the norm rather than the exception, and that it is more a statement of commitment and support than anything else.

Once this has been established and the work has started facilitators face one of their most important challenges, and this concerns the issue of dependency. It has already been said that the role is neither commonly used nor understood at first, so the natural reaction of our customers could well be to assume that if we are there to help, then that is what we should do, and that we should do it in the normal way which is to say what should be done. Most people are brought up with the view that help is something that is given directly and involves one person solving the other's problem, or at least saying how the problem should be solved: this, after all, is the traditional parental view. We have probably all been in this situation from both points of view, both as givers and recipients of such advice, and we therefore are aware of the possible reactions to this approach.

As recipients it all too often becomes clear to us that the other person either does not understand the situation, or at least has a very different interpretation of it than we do. This means that the help is often not very helpful. From the other perspective, as purveyors of advice and help, we often find that it is rejected, and we end up wondering why we bothered to give it in the first place. Though there are occasions when it works well, this approach tends not to be very successful as a way of changing behaviour, except in the short term when accompanied by other pressure, for example, 'Do this or I'll smack you!' or 'Do this or I'll sack you!'

There is another difficulty with this approach that is altogether more insidious. I am reminded of something that my grandfather used to say, which was, 'The trouble with gambling is that you might win!' The trouble with giving advice in this direct way is that people might accept it and then become dependent on us for giving it in the future. This runs counter to the whole idea of the facilitator role which concentrates attention on building self-sufficiency in those that we are working with, and ownership of the decisions that are made. The difficulty that many people have of course is that it makes us feel wanted and needed to be asked for help and advice, and so the giving of it helps to meet a need that we have, quite regardless of the situation of the other person. Most inexperienced facilitators find that they have to come to terms with this issue very soon after starting in the role, and so it is an important one to deal with straight away. The reality is that we will gain nothing by building dependent relationships, and we need to be sure that we are not doing so.

A second issue that needs to be explored is in some ways an extreme version of the dependency issue that has just been dealt with, and involves the temptation to 'do it yourself'. Properly selected facilitators are likely to be high achievers who are used to attaining goals and being successful. The facilitator role is designed to continue this, but to achieve successes through those that we are working with.

Whereas many of our customers will be similar in their motivation, it has to be said that there are those who are not, and there are yet others who, for whatever reason, find it difficult to achieve the improvements that are there for the taking. Sometimes this is to do with deficiencies in knowledge or skill, sometimes it seems more to do with the fear of the unknown and on other occasions it relates to a general inertia and lack of understanding of the possibilities that exist, but whatever the reason it can be very frustrating.

In such circumstances there is often the temptation to cut across the process and to become directly involved in doing the things that in fact our customers should be doing themselves. It is easy to succumb to the temptation of rationalizing this behaviour, but this is unlikely to help in anything other than appeasing our own desire for action. In practice we would be better occupied working out why our customer is having difficulties and trying to help the process of confronting the issues that are raised by this analysis.

A third issue of general importance concerns knowing when to 'back off'. As facilitators we are concerned with helping our customers to improve their performance either individually or in groups. There are occasions when this is by no means an easy task, and this can lead to the kind of frustration that is noted above. The temptation in these circumstances is often to continue 'pressurizing', and this is fine, up to a point. An important skill, however, is knowing when continuing the process will be counter-productive, and when it will be better to leave the discussion until a later date.

For all of us there are times when we are more energetic, imaginative and amenable than at others. If we are honest there are times when we would resist any attempt to influence us, simply because we felt 'bloody minded'. Knowing that we feel like this ourselves at times should give us an insight into situations when the same seems to be happening with our customers, and it should help us to deal with the situation in a sympathetic and sensitive way. Whereas we can gain credibility from knowing when it is sensible to accept that the time is not right, we will certainly lose out if we do not. This is not a recipe for avoiding necessary confrontation, it is a matter of being sensitive to the human realities that we are faced with. When we choose this response we should at the same time be clear in our own mind when and how we will revisit the issue.

The next general issue that should concern us is about preserving a balance in our approach between not accepting the *status quo* on the one hand, and not simply forcing the process to work, if it is being rejected for one reason or another. There will be occasions that we all come across as facilitators when those we are working with are either incapable of producing the results or refuse to. Though the skills we use are powerful, and will often produce surprising results, they are not a miraculous cure-all and there will be times when the obstacles are too great. We must beware of not accepting this too easily since remarkable results are often achieved in very difficult circumstances, but equally there is little to gain from forcing the process beyond its capability by a combination of 'bullying' and doing it ourselves. Indeed if we fall into this trap there is a danger that the word will spread and that it will contaminate our work in other potentially more rewarding circumstances.

Finally, as a general rule we should be careful that we are not becoming too involved in the task elements of the issues being dealt with by our customers. This is easy to say and much more difficult to do since we are brought up to be very task-oriented. We enjoy the satisfaction of solving a problem, of being able to think through issues and give good advice about precisely what should be done in a given situation. Being drawn too close to the particular issues will inevitably affect our ability to think clearly and impartially, and will tend to lead us into some or all of the traps that have been described above. Our role is to ask the questions that will help others to think things through, and this does not require us to have our perception of the answers to hand; in fact if we have we will be guilty of inappropriate manipulation. To perform our job successfully we have to be able to stand back from the precise issues or problems being dealt with.

There are, then, a number of general issues that the facilitator needs to take into account. Interestingly and importantly, these relate more to the traps that facilitators can fall into by being too concerned with meeting their own needs rather than those of their customers. It would be a rare person who was not in any way tempted to respond in the ways that have been discussed, and so the points raised are relevant to us all, and it is very important that we control the temptation to fulfil our own agendas at the expense of those of the individuals and groups that we are working with. Perhaps the golden rule in this is for us to keep the customer in the forefront of our minds, to develop a genuine feeling for their situation and to work from that starting point. If we constantly put ourselves in the other situation, see things as they see them, hear what they are saying, think in the way that they are thinking, we will be able to fulfil our role without diluting it in the ways that are described above.

17 Situations where facilitators are useful

Facilitators help people to be more effective than they would otherwise be by bringing to bear a knowledge and understanding of various aspects of individual and group behaviour, together with a range of practical skills, that liberate the true potential that exists in any given situation. It is a role that has many practical applications and as time goes by new ones will be tested and proved. At present most organizations have no understanding of the role itself and therefore do not understand its potential value, and among those that do have some knowledge the vast majority tend to use facilitators in what is, as yet, a rather stereotyped and limited way.

Problem-solving groups

Easily the most common use of the facilitator is in helping problem-solving groups with their work. The role is most usually introduced to an organization by outside consultants as an element of a process of change and improvement. Unfortunately many such consultants themselves have only a flimsy under-standing of the role and this often leads to facilitators being poorly trained and improperly used. None the less the most probable application is in this area.

Problem-solving groups are being used increasingly in organi-zations generally, and this is especially the case in those that are attempting to introduce concepts such as Total Quality, Business Process Re-engineering and so on. Similarly, those that are engaged in trying to promote team-building, employee involve-ment strategies and practical management development are likely to utilize group working as a main part of the particular initiative concerned.

Task forces of different kinds have been used for years, espe-cially by the more advanced and sophisticated organizations. Before the advent of the facilitator role these were sometimes very successful, sometimes an unmitigated disaster and some-times somewhere in between. The performance of such groups was usually evaluated in terms of the competence of the mem-bers. A successful group was assumed to have been so because there were good people in the group who knew what they were talking about, a disaster was explained away by rationalizing that the wrong people had been selected to be in the team or that they were not up to the task in the first place. In such organiza-tions the belief that 'two heads are better than one' was sufficient for them to continue with the approach, especially because fail-ures could so easily be rationalized away.

Our understanding of group dynamics and the subsequent development of the facilitator role, has transformed our under-standing of the true causes underlying success or failure and what can be done to manage such activities and increase their chances of success. Progressively organizations that have been exposed to the role, and which have developed even a rudimen-tary understanding of it, will tend to think of allocating a facilita-tor to new problem-solving groups, and those that have a deeper understanding of the power of the approach would not dream of establishing such an activity without one.

There are different types of problem-solving groups. Some are task forces, the members of which are selected, usually by senior management, to tackle a specific problem that affects the whole organization. These usually consist of members selected not only for their expertise in the particular subject, but also to reflect the different perceptions that exist in different departments or functions: they are deliberately selected with a cross-functional membership. Department groups are similar in the sense that the members are selected by management and that the problem is given to the group, but in this instance the main membership is from within one department or function. The dynamics of these two types of group will be different, influenced by many factors, including the fact that in a task force members may not know each other very well, if at all.

Another kind of problem-solving group is one made up of members of a natural working unit. If such a group was formed on the basis of voluntary membership it could be called a Quality Circle, but there are occasions when such an activity is made mandatory by the team leader. With groups where membership is voluntary the team has the responsibility for identifying the issue it wishes to address, which again has an effect on the dynamics that will have to be managed.

Finally, in more sophisticated organizations that have experience and skill in the use of group problem-solving, people are often empowered to set up cross-functional groups to address issues that concern them. Of course they work within an established set of guidelines, for example such groups would not deal with problems that were the natural preserve of someone else in the organization, or were to do with inappropriate subjects. For example a group of secretaries would not work on developing a five-year strategic plan for the business, neither would such a group deal with the issue of what should be the next pay award, but they may well be concerned enough about the system for travel requisitions, that affects them all, to want to tackle it.

Facilitators have a role to play in all these situations, first helping to make sure that the group understands the problem-solving process that should be used, second ensuring that the relevant techniques are applied rigorously and third assisting the leader and the members to manage the dynamics of the group successfully.

Individual situations

The understanding that properly-trained facilitators have of individual behaviour make them well-equipped to help individuals as well as groups. This is the second type of situation where facilitators can be used to good effect, though it is one that is very much under-used at present. The subject of training and development, and the best way of handling it, is one that is talked about constantly by those involved in developing and running such programmes. Increasingly, however, informed opinion believes that it needs to be geared specifically to the individual wherever possible, and that it needs to be based on an understanding of what is likely to motivate people to effective action that will help them to improve their performance.

Conventional wisdom says that, if it is to be cost-effective, training needs to be handled either by sending people to attend externally run courses or by putting everyone through internal programmes designed to meet the perceived generic needs of the organization. Paradoxically, conventional wisdom also has it that this approach is singularly unsuccessful in changing the behaviour of individuals in any practical sense. Thus this approach is cost-efficient rather than cost-effective, and though there will always be a place for traditional training courses, there is a need for more effective approaches.

The difficulties of arranging training and development at the individual level are obvious: it is likely to cost more and it may well stretch the available resources that are required to the point that not everyone will be able to be accommodated, unless, that is, trained facilitators acting in a part-time capacity are deployed to meet the requirement. Individual approaches will be more sensitive to personal needs and wants, therefore the potential for using trained and skilled facilitators in individual training and development represents one of the most exciting developments in this field that there has been for many years.

As more and more organizations recognize the requirement for continuous improvement both at an organizational and an individual level, it becomes a crucial ingredient in any change process that people receive enough help and support at a personal level to make sure that individual improvement really does happen. Even with trained facilitators available it is probable in organizations of any size that not everyone will be able to receive the necessary support at the same time.

Where this is the case, senior managers should be the first 'target audience' since it is their example that will have an important influence on others. Using a trained and skilled facilitator to help senior people work through what they can do to improve, and how they should go about doing it, seems in practice to be a prerequisite for their active involvement in personal improvement.

To put it bluntly, experience indicates that, if left alone, people at the senior level are, for the most part, highly unlikely to personalize the message of improvement that they are sending out to the organization at large. They are much more likely to spend their time doing just the same as they have always done, after all, they were the activities that made them successful in the first place and complaining that no-one else seems to be committing themselves to the necessary improvements that are so obvious!

Skilled facilitation is virtually always necessary to avoid this paralysing situation, and it is encouraging to see that an increasing number of senior managers, especially from the more advanced and sophisticated organizations, are choosing to deploy a facilitator to help them. If senior management does not play its part and change its behaviour, the people in the organization will notice that the message appears to be 'do as I say, not as I do', and will tend to the view that they will become interested and do something about it as and when they see some demonstrable evidence of commitment from the top, in the form of behaviour rather than just fine words.

The involvement of facilitators in problem-solving groups and their help with individual development is usually associated, as has already been said, with organization-wide improvement initiatives. It is perhaps revealing that only very infrequently is it recognized that the role can be of just as much value in assisting with 'normal' meetings. Managers spend much of their time in this mode. Some people become very frustrated by this and complain that they spend so much time in meetings that they have no time left to do any 'real work'. Though faintly amusing, and amazingly common, this reaction shows a remarkable lack of understanding of what the manager is there to do.

Organizations of any size are complex. Decisions have to be made which balance different perceptions and requirements. Limited resources of people, capital and time have to be deployed to best effect and in the recognition that any course of action is likely to have an effect on other parts of the business. Plans have to be made that take into account the whole, not just the constituent parts. If these things are not necessary then why have managers, and if they are then how is such work to be done if not through a process of meeting and discussion?

In fact the reaction is caused not by having meetings *per se*, but by the fact that so many meetings are conducted so appallingly badly that those involved become intensely frustrated and de-motivated by them and blame the meeting itself rather than the fact that it was not run well. Trained facilitators know all too well that this happens, and they also know the reasons why. It is rarely to do with any lack of technical knowledge among those attending or indeed is it normally the case that the meeting should not have been held.

The issue, nine times out of ten, concerns the process or dynamics of the group concerned. It could be the behaviour of the chairperson or other group members; it could be the lack of balance in team roles; it could be the lack of a clear definition of the purpose of the meeting, 'groupthink', 'the Abilene paradox', and so on. Actually it is likely to be a range of issues that, because the group does not understand group behaviour, it is simply incapable of managing.

In every organization meetings are held to do with subjects and decisions that are vital to future survival and success and they are often managed in a way that we would hope that our deadliest competitors are conducting theirs, since if this were the case it would make our job much easier! Using the knowledge and skills of facilitators helps to avoid this dreadfully dangerous situation and demonstrates that the role should not just be confined to what, up until now, has been its conventional uses.

Most organizations face crises from time to time: events that have to be handled with extreme delicacy and care if they are to be confronted or circumnavigated successfully. It is during these times that normally sane and sound people can display the most remarkable lack of judgement. The Bay of Pigs fiasco which has been mentioned elsewhere in this book is a case in point. Again the potential problem will probably be more to do with the group's lack of knowledge of the issues that are affecting its work, and therefore its inability to manage the process success-fully, than any lack of technical ability on the part of the mem-bers. If there is one type of situation where the involvement of a trained facilitator should be absolutely compulsory it is this, and yet one wonders how often this is the case even in organizations that are well-used to the role. It is a strange omission, and one that leads me to the view that even where the role is known, understood and used, the chances are that facilitators are associ-ated with whatever initiative is being introduced, and that most people in the organization see this as being separate and apart from the important business of running the company, rather than as the normal way that they want the organization to do its business. Tragic but true.

Thus far we have considered the possible uses of trained facili-tators in working with groups of different kinds, and with indi-viduals. It is also the case, in this world of massive change, that help is needed with the thinking through, structuring, planning, development and ongoing support for the process of change and development that is necessary for the survival and success of organizations everywhere.

Facilitators in this role will normally be working with the senior management team and, for the most part, the people that are used to do this will tend to be brought in from the outside, either in the form of consultants or by employing someone who has been involved in such a change process in another organiza-tion. This second approach is worth a word of warning, since facilitating a process such as this is very different from having been a part of it as one of the management team, even if the role was a coordinating one. It is a course of action that can work, but all too often it does not. There is nothing to stop enthusiastic facilitators from embarking on a programme of self-develop-

ment that will ultimately equip them to be able to work successfully in this area, but it should be recognized that more than just
a basic level of knowledge and skills will be needed.

When working with the senior team in this way, a slightly different approach is needed which combines the roles of 'expert'
and 'process' consultant. It can be quite tricky to get the balance
right and so it will be worth exploring it, at least in outline.

At this level one of the issues that needs to be addressed is the
planning of the stages of the entire change process. There is no
doubt that a knowledge of how such processes work in practice
is very useful in determining what should be done.
Unfortunately it is usually the case that only the consultant or
facilitator has this knowledge. It is also unquestionable that the
ownership of the plan must reside with the senior team rather
than with those that are advising them.

The challenge then is clear, to enable the team to make a good
set of decisions that they own fully. The keys to the facilitator's
approach in this situation should be in examples and illustrations, in the first instance, rather than in giving direct and
prescriptive advice, and wherever possible in giving viable alter-
natives for the group to assess and to choose from.

Though the primary concern of this book is the use of the facilitator within the context of organizations, it would be remiss not
to mention the potential for using facilitator skills in situations
outside work. The knowledge and skills covered in this book can
readily be seen as essential ingredients for living a full, productive, psychologically healthy and helpful life. There are countless
examples of facilitators who tell their own particular stories of
how they have used their facilitative skills in a whole variety of
situations outside work, and have found that they are just as
powerful.

One person attended an MRA International facilitator course
in Ireland. The very next week he was walking home when he
came across someone who was about to commit suicide by
jumping off a bridge. After having recovered from an immediate
attack of panic, he tells the story of how he used the skills he had
learned on the course to talk this person out of jumping, and of
his elation when he succeeded.

Being a committed facilitator seems to transcend the formal occasions where the role is used, and for many it permeates every aspect of life.

18 Case histories in facilitation

It is always useful in gaining an insight into a new subject to be able to refer to examples and this chapter meets this requirement. Facilitators are now being used in an increasing number of situations and the case histories examined here reflect this.

Case 1   Facilitating a problem-solving group

The situation
The leader and the group in this case were very impatient. They had short-circuited the problem-solving process, had gone straight to possible solutions and believed that they had completed their work after only four weeks. The facilitator, who had missed two of the four meetings that the group had held, could see that this was not so, but was faced with three issues. First, the group was very pleased with itself and she had the challenge of telling them that they had not addressed the problem thoroughly without losing their commitment. The second issue

163

concerned the ego of the leader. This person was noted for rushing at things and was proud of his 'get things done' attitude. He had only attended half of the leader training course because 'there were important things to be done in the department' and he believed that he could not afford the time for the training. Third, it was clear that the group had not used the problem-solving process.

The approach

The facilitator decided that she should avoid any confrontation with the group and work through the leader. She arranged a planning meeting and started by stressing the gains that the group had made. She suggested that the leader start the next meeting by tabling these benefits and congratulating the group. The leader thought that this was a good idea.

The facilitator then made the point that she did not believe that the group had finished its task. She explained that she thought they had rather leapt to conclusions without identifying the root cause of the problem. The leader was quite defensive about this feedback so the facilitator asked him to take her through the problem-solving cycle and to explain the different techniques that the group had used and what had come out of them. The fact that the leader could not do this adequately helped to make the point.

It would have been easy for the facilitator to antagonize the leader at this point, so she took a positive line and asked if it was possible that the group could have achieved more out of the already good work that they had done. She also stressed how important was the leader's role in encouraging the group to use the structure fully and properly and made the point that she was sure that they would follow his lead if he encouraged them to explore the issue more fully.

The leader received this feedback and accepted that more could be achieved, and so did the group when it was put to them. They began to use the problem-solving process rigorously and were able to solve a very serious problem that had been limiting their ability to produce their product. They now consistently meet and exceed their production targets, which they had never been able to do before. In addition the leader of the group has improved his managerial performance significantly.

Assessment
An important first point is that the facilitator missed an early group meeting and that the leader arranged a further meeting without her. This was probably significant in creating the situation that emerged. There are countless examples of this kind of thing happening. The leader and the group were still not clear enough about what the facilitator was there to do, and felt that they could solve their problem themselves without any guidance. Once this had happened, the leader and the group were always going to be defensive about a later intervention since they, inevitably, would become protective of their work. This could be seen as a dimension of groupthink with the group displaying selective perception and rejecting information that did not concur with their own current perception.

This example helps to reinforce the point that facilitators do need to attend group meetings, at least for the first full problem-solving cycle. None the less the facilitator recovered and her success in this situation was due to her ability to give feedback in a non-judgemental way, and to nurture both the leader and the group by stressing the good work that they had done and using this to encourage them to build on it.

She was wise in working through the leader to achieve this, since had she gone straight to the group she would probably have encountered 'subgrouping' with her in a subgroup of one, faced with the collective rationalizations of everyone else. Having the leader committed to the course of action was crucial, as was working through him in addressing the issue with the group.

Case 2   Facilitating Statistical Process Control

The situation
A food processing factory had decided to apply Statistical Process Control (SPC) to their production lines. Training had

been given to the operators and the system had been put in place, but without the use of a facilitator. In the course of doing his work it became clear to the facilitator that many of the operators were filling in the charts incorrectly and, what was worse, they were doing it on purpose.

He was told that the operators feared being reprimanded for poor results. The training that the operators had received had dealt with their responsibilities for filling out the charts, but it had not gone into the underlying philosophy of SPC as a mechanism to give the operator more control over the process and the opportunity to work on improving it. Management did not have sufficient understanding of SPC either, because it seemed clear that they were indeed using the results to criticize the operators rather than the production process itself. The operators, being sensible people, quickly learned avoidance techniques, in this case, to falsify the results to make them appear satisfactory.

It was clear to the facilitator that something had to be done about the situation, but he was concerned about how to do it. On the one hand he could have collected the evidence of falsifying the figures and used it to confront managers, but this risked a loss of confidence and a negative backlash from the operators and management alike. Alternatively he could try a more general approach that did not use the falsified figures directly. This approach depended for success on a higher level of facilitative skill, but was the option he chose.

The approach
The facilitator decided to arrange a meeting to review progress with SPC, and used it to discuss people's attitude to the technique and also whether the organization was achieving the best results possible from it. The discussion was free-flowing and quite lively at times, and the facilitator had to use his skills to avoid it becoming too personal as many of the managers were keen to rationalize their behaviour. In the end they achieved agreement on three points:

1   SPC is about examining and improving work processes, not testing and blaming individuals.

2   Managers have to facilitate the introduction and mainte-
    nance of the technique for it to stand any chance of lasting
    success.
3   Operators must be encouraged to share in the responsibility
    of understanding and improving the process, and have to
    feel that they can alert managers to difficulties if this is going
    to happen.

Following this meeting the facilitator arranged individual sessions with each of the managers concerned, and used these meetings to create action plans including an agreed amount of
support from the facilitator in the forthcoming few weeks.

Within three months both managers and operators had developed a new-found confidence both in each other and in the use
of the SPC system. Tangible results were being achieved regularly and a sense of real partnership was being developed. The
facilitator arranged to hold regular review meetings to ensure
that the issues of support and mutual· confidence were main-
tained as well as the mechanics of the system.

The facilitator was also anxious to be sure that ample recognition was given to all parties consistently during this stage. With
this in mind he made sure that a range of people, from the managing director down, knew of the gains that were being made,
and made sure that they gave appropriate recognition both to
the operators and the managers concerned, in both formal and
informal settings.

Assessment
A common feature of working as a facilitator is that, since we
generally speaking have no direct line relationship with people
we tend to be seen as non-threatening. This means that we can
become privy to views that are kept from the managers who so
often, as in this case, represent authority and punishment. The
difficulty we face in such circumstances is that managers tend
not to accept this view of themselves and they certainly do not
like the idea that things could be being done behind their backs
without their knowing it.

From the other perspective we have to be careful about

'spilling the beans', especially if this includes naming names, since this would cause people to question their trust in us. All in all, in situations like this we have to use our facilitator skills if we are going to end up with anyone at all being prepared to talk to us!

In this case the facilitator's success was due to his ability to separate the idea of improvement from the issue of individual criticism and blame. The managers thus found it much easier to support the actions that were agreed. It is important, as well, to note that the agreed actions are all expressed in the positive: they are building and developing statements, very different for example from an action which said, 'we will stop punishing operators for poor results'. In fact it is unlikely that such a statement would ever have been agreed, the argument would probably still be going on today.

In addition to this the facilitator was quite clever in being able to confront the situation by not confronting it. A more direct approach would probably have led to defensiveness and acrimony and could well have made things even worse than they were. By concentrating on the way ahead, and the opportunities for making things even better, a positive climate was created.

Finally, but certainly not least in importance, the issue of recognition was not missed. It is so easy to forget this vital ingredient, or to assume that it will happen naturally. It hardly ever does, at least in the estimation of those who are involved. Because of this it needs to be orchestrated, and the facilitator arranged this well.

Case 3   Facilitation in negotiating requirements

The situation
This case comes from a health authority that had decided to introduce a technique called the In-Department Evaluation of Activities (IDEA), which is a way of negotiating requirements between internal suppliers and customers.

In one particular department there were a number of issues

that could have made this both difficult and dangerous. In thinking about the approach the facilitator was particularly concerned with three issues. First, informal discussions with some of this particular team revealed that they felt that the manager was out of touch with reality. The manager thought that the department gave excellent service, whereas they could see that this was not so, a view which was strongly supported by the customers. Second the customers had said privately that they intended to use the IDEA process to expose the manager and the poor level of service being given, and third there were two people in the eight-person team who were so demotivated that they said that they wanted nothing to do with the technique, or anything else for that matter.

The approach

The first important decision that the facilitator made was consciously not to make assumptions about what would happen as IDEA was introduced. On the basis of the information she had been given, it would have been all too easy to have become overly defensive and so to have 'contaminated' the approach.

At the first meeting of the department there was considerable and quite acrimonious feedback about the view expressed by some of the team; that the manager did not listen, and how some of the work done in the department was unnecessary. One person refused to become involved at all.

After this meeting the manager went to the senior management team in their capacity as the steering group for the overall improvement process. He said that he had talked to his team: that they had found the meeting too uncomfortable and that they wanted to stop the process since it was ruining team spirit. When this became known, some of the team members went to see the facilitator and disassociated themselves from what the manager had said. They explained that they wanted to continue since they were starting to deal with real issues at last, even though it was a bit painful.

The facilitator then went to the steering group and put the case for continuing, which they agreed with on the basis that a decision to stop should not be made after only one meeting. So the facilitator had to meet with the manager, both to plan this and also to rebuild their relationship.

They met and had a frank and open discussion. The facilitator encouraged the leader to express his concerns, and to examine why he had moved from a positive to a negative stance concerning the IDEA process. She listened carefully. He explained that it was him rather than the staff who had wanted to stop, and that this was because he was concerned about losing control. He said that he had felt intimidated by some of the things that team members had said about him and the department, and he expressed great concern about the negotiation meetings with customers that are a key part of IDEA, since he knew in his heart of hearts that all was not well.

The facilitator stressed the key notion of improvement rather than protection of the *status quo*, and put the view that this was what would be valued in the future. She continued by stressing the strength and the underlying commitment of the team, and reinforced the point that the steering group were hoping for a real success in using IDEA in his department which would give both him and the team a lot of recognition.

The process was started again with the full backing of the manager. Some of the customer negotiation meetings were indeed quite difficult, but the manager and the team did not, for the most part, become defensive.

One main output of the process was that the department reorganized itself to be far more customer-oriented. The whole group involved itself in a presentation to the steering group which was very well received. As a part of the presentation the department committed itself to using the IDEA process each year to be sure that they were really continuing to adapt successfully to changing customer requirements. The group also decided to continue with weekly meetings as an internal team-building mechanism.

Assessment
In the early stages the facilitator was instrumental in setting up a situation that was fraught and difficult, which is interesting especially since she had recognized the potential danger before

she started. She was certainly not successful in creating a positive frame of mind for the manager. Maybe she should have done some more work with him before setting up the first meeting, or at least she could have prepared him better for the meeting by taking him through the stages of group development. This would have helped to 'displace' the likely feedback somewhat, while still having it available to be used. In practice the reaction was defensive in the extreme. Certainly she needed a lot of facilitative skill to get the process back on track.

During her meeting with the leader the facilitator had to spend most of her time eliciting and listening, and she seems to have done well in this. There was a point during this meeting when the leader, having accepted the point about improvement rather than the *status quo*, was becoming more able and willing to express his worries about what the process would reveal and what this would say about him as a manager.

This often happens and from the facilitator's point of view there are two issues to be considered at this point. First, the fact of bringing the leader to this stage was attributable to good facilitation, but second there is always a danger that the concerns that begin to pour out begin to frighten the leader again and cause a 'relapse' expressed in the form of rationalizations. From the facilitator's point of view there can be a temptation to allow the leader to continue too long in this mode, since it is an expression of what the facilitator has been trying to do, but to let it go too far is both unnecessary and self-indulgent on the part of the facilitator.

In this case the facilitator saw that she did not need the leader to continue in this mode: all she wanted was for him to agree, willingly, to continue with the process and to commit himself to working with his team to get the best out of it in terms of improvement. This was an example of good and sensitive facilitation.

Case 4 Facilitators and management development

The situation
An improvement process had been established for two years, and having gained a range of successes with it, the steering group decided that the whole of the management development process needed to be seen and structured within this context.

During the initial training that had been implemented two years earlier, the Hersey and Blanchard Situational Leadership model had been described and all managers had completed a questionnaire that gives feedback about perceptions of leader style from the perspective of the managers themselves. This model is described in the Appendix (see pp. 193–201).

The senior team wanted to take this process further and to develop more effective management styles themselves and in the rest of the management team but saw that skilled facilitation would be needed to cause this to happen.

The approach
As well as gathering self-perception feedback, it is possible to use the Situational Leadership model to gather information from the boss, subordinates and peers: to compare this with the self-assessment and to use it as the basis of individual improvement plans. This was the selected approach and three internal facilitators were chosen, and trained, for this particular role as internal management developers. One of the first decisions they made was that they themselves would meet regularly and try to learn from each other's experience

It was recognized that this approach needed to be seen as a medium- to long-term initiative and so the plan called for individual meetings between a facilitator and a manager on a monthly basis for the forthcoming year. It was estimated that the initial two to three meetings would take up to three hours, but that after this first stage, one-hour meetings would be sufficient in most instances.

The basic information was collected by asking the boss, up to six subordinates and up to four peers, to complete a question-naire about the leadership behaviour of the person concerned. This was administered by the facilitator so that individual feed-back could remain anonymous.

The three facilitators were strongly advised to set the context for the activity as one of the need for every employee to be actively and constantly working on a programme of personal improvement. To reinforce the point it was arranged that the managing director was among the first people to become involved. While a few managers were defensive at the start, most welcomed the opportunity when they realized that it was designed for everyone, and that it bore no implied criticism of what they had been doing to date.

Gathering and using feedback in this way had a number of interesting and useful benefits. First, it gave managers, for the first time, orderly and non-emotive feedback about how others saw their behaviour. Once the initial temptation to reject differ-ent views as wrong or misguided had been overcome, it was seen as a great opportunity to understand different reactions and to be more sensitive to the individuals that the managers were dealing with.

Second, this mechanism gave people a simple and under-standable language to use when discussing the issues of man-agement style and approach. The benefit of this was that it became possible to have sane, intelligent discussions about what had in the past been seen as a dangerous, and sometimes taboo, subject. Many of the managers began to have regular meetings with their teams, first to explain the model and the 'language', and then to encourage a sharing of views about which styles were the most appropriate to use in different situations that indi-viduals and the group faced.

One of the most important results of this whole process was that many of the managers were able to measure the improve-ments in their performance. This was made possible largely because they were encouraged to set themselves tangible improvement goals, where the issue of leadership style was a relevant factor, rather than dealing with the issue of style in a general and unspecified sense.

The success of this approach led to the decision to extend it to include team leaders and key personnel as the next stage. Over half the managers also asked for the sessions with their facilitator to continue albeit at a reduced frequency.

Assessment
Because there were three facilitators involved, and a number of individual managers, it is not possible to analyse their performance in detail. However, it is evident that the exercise was a success

During the regular meetings with the managers, the facilitators had to use many of the skills that are covered in this book, and they had to be particularly careful that the ownership of the improvement process, and people's plans, was with the person concerned rather than themselves. They were able to achieve this.

A final point is that the facilitators, from the outset, could have taken an individualistic and competitive stance, but they chose rather to work together and to learn from each other. There is no doubt that this decision will have benefited their individual performance as they learned about different possible ways of handling different situations. Furthermore it will have widened the range of options that they have available to them when facilitating in the future. It will also have made the whole experience less daunting and more fun.

In any organization where there is more than one person in the facilitator role, whether full- or part-time, it is well worth noting that others in the same circumstances have always found it extremely valuable to meet, to share experiences and to continue the process of learning and developing together.

Case 5   Facilitation and the steering group

In this case the organization concerned had been working with an external consultancy for three years, establishing and consolidating the first stages of a comprehensive, organization-wide improvement process. Many gains had been made and the facilitators within the company were largely self-sufficient with the basic tools. With the active support of the consultant the steering group wanted to go to the next step in developing their own self-sufficiency in managing the whole process by themselves, so it was agreed that the consultant should phase out of attending the monthly planning and review meetings. Historically the role of the outside adviser had involved not only providing guidance in the structuring of the initiative but also helping the group with the process of their meetings which had been poor at the start.

The approach
The danger of the consultant ceasing attendance at the meetings was that the group would lapse back into old habits but would not be prepared to admit and deal with the situation. The need for a facilitator was discussed openly and the decision was made that someone from within the group should be given the role, rather than one of the trained internal facilitators, since it was felt that at that stage anyone other than a complete and impartial outsider may well find the task too difficult.

Fortunately two of the steering group had been trained as facilitators, so it was agreed that one of them would act as the group's 'process consultant' while the other would have regular planning and review meetings with him to discuss progress. It was also agreed that they should keep in touch with the external consultant and that he should receive a copy of the minutes of the meetings at least for the time being.

At the first meeting without the consultant the challenge facing the group was discussed openly and every individual expressed their commitment to the organization's philosophy and to playing their part in ensuring continued success. Over the following months two things emerged as being significant. The first was that the facilitator, recognizing the importance of the way that the group was working, placed great store by the process reviews that he conducted at the end of every meeting. From the outset he was less willing to intervene in the meeting itself to make process points, something that he later explained was due to a lack of confidence in his skills.

This led to a situation where, though the subject of the way that the group was working was discussed, the experience became frustrating because it was happening after the event when it was too late to do anything about it. One director summed-up the view of the majority when she said in one process review that they must develop the skill and the courage to deal with these issues at the time if they were to develop into a truly effective, interdependent team. The group gave encouragement to the facilitator to help them, while at the same time recognizing their own individual responsibility.

The second issue of significance concerned the question of which new tools and techniques should be used to meet the problems and opportunities that were constantly being uncovered. Progressively the group realized that they did not always have the knowledge to be able to make wise choices and that this was a legitimate area for the continued use of an external adviser. This was brought home to them when a situation arose in the Research and Development department that needed addressing. They simply did not know what to do, whereas when they called their consultant he was very quickly able to see that the situation was ideal for the use of Taguchi's experimental designs. A training programme was arranged and soon the issue was being dealt with.

To start with the team had felt reluctant to call their consultant, thinking that this in some way was indicative of their failing to manage the process themselves. In fact it is an example of the need to keep in touch with relevant technical knowledge that exists outside the organization, whatever the issue being tackled. This group has continued to meet successfully and over a period of time individual members have taken more responsibility for the group's process, rather than simply leaving this aspect to the facilitator.

Assessment

With regard to facilitator skills the first point is that senior groups need facilitators just as much as others, in fact in my experience they tend to need them even more. The second point is that it is perfectly possible for trained internal facilitators to work with groups at any level. Though in this case a member of the group was given the job, a more junior person would have been just as successful given the required facilitator training.

As far as the facilitator's performance in this case is concerned a key point concerns the place of the process review at the end of group meetings. Before facilitators are introduced into organizations people tend to know nothing of process, let alone the idea of process reviews. In the early stages it is easier, and more convenient to deal with process issues at the end of the meeting, since to do it during proceedings can result in confusing and frustrating the group. As knowledge of this important area, and skill in highlighting and addressing key issues of group dynamics increases, it becomes more possible to deal with them efficiently during the normal course of the meetings.

For a variety of reasons, not least his lack of confidence at the outset, the facilitator did not do this until the group had become frustrated enough to raise the issue. It is a challenge for all facilitators to be able to intervene appropriately and effectively during the course of the meetings themselves, and it is a skill which tends to be developed in line with the increased confidence that comes from a few successful experiences in the role. Even where issues are being addressed during the meeting, there should still be a process review at the end, although it will usually be shorter than before.

Another issue is the ability to recognize the situations where outside knowledge or experience is needed. Facilitators must avoid putting themselves in the role of the fount of all knowledge from outside the group, which can sometimes be a seductive option. Furthermore they will often have an important job to do, not only in encouraging the group to seek outside views nondefensively, but also as 'resource investigators' in finding where the particular outside expertise can be found and in involving it appropriately.

19 Choosing the correct approach

It goes without saying that it will be important for facilitators to think carefully about, and to select the most appropriate way of structuring their approach to the people they are working with, whether they be individuals or groups. There are some general rules regarding this, and there are a number of other considerations that relate more to the individual nature of the customers.

At the outset, whether working with individuals or in groups, the role of the facilitator must be described at least in outline. There are three key issues that need to be covered in such an introduction. First, it should be made clear that the ownership of the activity lies with the individual or group concerned, and not with the facilitator. This is always necessary because the role itself is unusual in most organizations, where being involved, especially in an apparently 'leading' or at least influential position, is generally taken to indicate ownership.

The second point is that the main job of the facilitator is to help the group or individual in whatever way is necessary to achieve self-sufficiency. This must be put in carefully chosen words since it is not meant to imply any present incompetence. Typically at this point we would stress the value of having different tools and techniques available. We would suggest that we can help by passing these over as they are needed, and by helping the individual or group as they use them up to the point when they feel confident that they can proceed unaided. If necessary the point can be made that people learn best by doing, and that the facilitator role puts this principle into practice.

The issue of task and process is the next one to be explained. Because most people are almost entirely task-oriented, as opposed to process-oriented, there will be a natural expectation that anyone who is involved, whatever their title, will contribute directly to the task at hand. If someone avoids this without any explanation, it will certainly lead to confusion, and probably frustration and annoyance as well. If this happens, then work on the task will inevitably be affected to the detriment of all, and to the certain diminution of the facilitator's effectiveness. The point, then, should be reinforced that it is not our job to solve the problem or to decide what to do, that is the task of the individual or team.

Our job is to give whatever help is needed in the way the task is approached. This can be through providing information and training in useful tools and techniques: with groups it will also include helping to make sure that the way the members are working together is effective, and with individuals it will also include the opportunity for bouncing ideas and possibilities off someone who can view the situation dispassionately.

Facilitators work with individuals in the role of developer. Sometimes this is a purely individual process, and on other occasions it involves leaders of problem-solving groups. Facilitators also attend problem-solving or other group meetings. When dealing with leaders of problem-solving groups, the 'three-meeting structure' is the most effective general approach. It has been used all over the world to great effect. Where it is used, it works, where it is not used, facilitators find it much more difficult to be effective, and so it is a general principle that we should not deviate from.

The three meetings, conducted well, ensure a cycle of continuous improvement that is one of the main benefits of having facilitators involved. The cycle can be summarized as: plan, meet, review.

The planning meeting is held between the facilitator and the leader, and takes about 30 minutes. It is, as it sounds, the opportunity to think through what are the objectives of the next meeting of the group and how these will be realized. Though it is obvious that the quality of a meeting will largely depend on the quality of the preparation that has gone into it, it is none the less the case that all too often meetings are ill prepared and hence are not effective, or indeed efficient. Ask managers to list their problems and the things that could be improved and, quite regardless of industry or culture, many of them are likely to mention either that there are too many meetings, or that the meetings they attend are a waste of time.

This situation is immortalized in the John Cleese video *Meetings, Bloody Meetings*. When asked by his wife why he has to bring his work home with him, his response is that he has no time to do it while at work because he is always in meetings. When it is suggested that surely the meetings are held to conduct work, the response is a dismissive snort and a statement that you don't work in meetings, you just . . . well . . . meet! The fact that the video has been used all over the world as a training mechanism for conducting effective meetings suggests that there is a big requirement to improve this area of management competence, and it is this that the preparation meetings are designed to do.

At the preparation meeting the main objective is to plan and structure the forthcoming meeting of the group. This involves more than simply saying what we want to achieve since our ability to do so will be influenced by the skill that is displayed in managing the process of the group's work. Because of this one of the key parts of the planning meeting will concern itself with discussing the important dynamics that affected the last group meeting and exploring ways of eradicating negative parts of the process and reinforcing positive elements. This will include issues such as the balance of contributions and any particularly influential behaviours on the part of group members. If, for example, one person seemed to be dominating the proceedings in a way that was not helpful, a part of the plan might well be how the leader should handle the situation if it occurred again. Similarly if one person had withdrawn from the work of the group at the last meeting it will be necessary to have a strategy for avoiding this in the future or dealing with it if it did happen again. Picking up the important process issues from the previous meeting and agreeing how to handle them is, therefore, just as important a part of the preparation meeting as is the content.

As far as content is concerned the plan needs to build in any training that might be necessary to give the group access to a technique that will help them get to the next stage. A main principle of using facilitators in group situations is that since people learn best by doing and that immediate practice and reinforcement is easily the best approach, the facilitator should be able to train group members in the use of different techniques during the course of the meetings themselves and that the technique should then be used as a part of the same meeting. Since the meetings should last no longer than an hour, or one and a half hours as an absolute maximum, careful planning is always needed so that both training, if this is needed, and also putting the technique into practice can be achieved in the same meeting.

Another important element of the planning process involves ensuring that demonstrable progress is being made from meeting to meeting. This is necessary because people in group situations are often impatient and want to be able to see that they are indeed going forward. If they feel that they are not, there is a danger that they will very quickly develop the perception that the group is merely a 'talking shop', and if this happens it is difficult to shift this view. It is always better to ensure that demonstrable progress is being made, and to reinforce the point at group meetings as one way of keeping the motivation of the group at a high level.

Finally, the planning meeting is designed to ensure that the administrative requirements for the meeting are thought through. There is nothing worse than going to a one-hour meeting, finding out in the first five minutes that there is no flip chart and that the marker pens are dry and then having to spend 20 minutes solving this problem rather than the one that the group has been formed to address.

Since facilitators will be holding planning meetings routinely as a part of their role, it makes sense to design a simple form which can be used to record the decisions made at the meeting. This also has the advantage of acting as a record and a reference if the meeting goes off track. Since it is the leader's rather than the facilitator's meeting the leader should be the one who fills out the form, which will be a useful discipline even after the facilitator has withdrawn on the basis of the self-sufficiency of the leader.

The second event in the three-meeting structure is the meeting of the group itself where the plan will be put into operation. Facilitators should attend these meetings and should operate in the role of process observers and also potentially of trainers, if this is needed because of any lack in the confidence or ability of the leader. In the former role it is important that we work hard to understand the group dynamics issues that are particularly affecting the work of the group. Because so much happens in the course of a one-hour meeting it makes sense for facilitators to note down the most important things, since these will be the main input to the review meeting that follows.

The third meeting is held between the leader and the facilitator and represents the main opportunity for us to help the leader analyse how the meeting went, learn from it and to construct an improvement plan. Unless this is handled well, not only will we have missed an opportunity, we will call into question the validity of using facilitators in the first place. The review meeting should have as its output an action plan that will help the leader to focus attention on the key issues that will contribute to an improved performance. The plan, if it is to be really effective, needs to be owned by the leader rather than the facilitator, and so we need to use our skills at helping people to think through their performance and converting the issues that are raised into appropriate actions. Little will be achieved if we merely conduct an appraisal of performance and expect the leader to act on it.

PART V
Management Style

For the most part the way that facilitators have been used to date has been to support individuals and groups, and to do this from a position that is separate from the line management process. That this is necessary calls into question the effectiveness of many managers when it comes to the development of their people. In an ideal world the manager would *be* the facilitator, and it is therefore relevant to address the issue here.

There is little doubt that a raised level of expectations concerning what work should provide for the individual, changes the nature of the manager's job, and means that different approaches and a higher level of skill are required to fulfil the role successfully. The principles and practice of facilitation can be of enormous benefit to managers everywhere, and this is the subject of Part V.

20 Facilitation as a management style

There is a view emerging among many management thinkers that facilitative management styles, if they are understood clearly, and practised with skill, hold the key to performing this complex and demanding role. The Hersey and Blanchard Situational Leadership model, described in detail in the Appendix, is the best for understanding this process.

There have been many contributions to the subject of management and leadership style over the years, but they have often served to frustrate managers rather than help them because, for the most part, they imply that there is one, all-purpose, ideal style that we should aspire to. This makes no sense to anyone who is responsible for a range of different people. To illustrate the point, anyone who has more than one child knows that it would be crazy to 'manage' them in exactly the same way. We have to be sensitive to the individual quirks and needs, abilities and expectations of the individual child. Furthermore, I am acutely aware that my own children 'manage' myself and my wife differently, and intuitively in ways that are most likely to achieve what they want: 'out of the mouths of babes and sucklings'!

One of the main difficulties, historically, has been the rigidity of the styles used by many managers. Without a simple-to-use conceptual and practical framework, people have little option but to behave in the way that comes naturally to them. This will be influenced by their beliefs and expectations, but the result tends to be a style that has little to do with the particular situation of the people being managed. Because of this the approach is likely to work on some occasions and to be a disaster on others. In this latter situation the manager tends to justify the outcome with accusations of negative attitudes and intransigence.

Discussions of management style often revolve round arguments about the appropriateness of authoritarian approaches as opposed to those that are more consultative and participative. In fact any rigid formula will be successful on some occasions, but not on others. Participation does not always work any more than autocracy or paternalism, which is why a more sensitive and flexible approach is required. This need is made more important and urgent as people are less and less prepared to be treated as automatons, and as the fast-changing nature of our world requires that we are able to encourage the best out of people in what is often a bewildering array of different situations. It is made even more essential as we realize the true cost of not doing so. Have you ever been managed by someone who, in your view, used the wrong style? And what was the result? Frustration, confusion, demotivation, reduction in performance and so on – the consequences are real and profound.

This is why more sensitive, facilitative approaches, based on the principle of managing according to the precise situation, hold the key for the future. Managers, in general, seem to find it easy to understand the Hersey and Blanchard model and most see it as potentially useful since it appeals to common sense as well as matching their experience. The important conceptual features of this way of viewing the challenge of management and leadership are that it says that the right style is a function of the situation and that the situation is defined by the person being managed or led rather than the natural abilities or inclinations of the leader.

In addition the model is developmental; it does not assume a static situation, rather it calls for active effort on the part of the leader to develop the ability and willingness of the follower and then to utilize a different style to reflect this change. Importantly the approach also covers the eventuality of a regression in ability and/or willingness, so it is 'client-centred'.

The Situational Leadership model deals with one of the difficulties that many managers have in approaching their complex and demanding role, which is that most have no clear view of how they should be approaching the job other than behaving in the way that feels most comfortable to them based on their own natural inclinations. In other words most managers use a style or styles that suit themselves, rather than the situation they find themselves in judged by the level of ability and willingness of the person they are managing. Sometimes the style used will work, but on other occasions it will not and there will be no immediately apparent reason for the difference. So often in these circumstances the manager rationalizes what happens by referring to negativity on the part of the person being managed rather than to a failure to use the appropriate style for the particular situation.

Situational Leadership provides a very useful conceptual framework for any manager to understand that the styles used need to relate to the level of ability and willingness of the follower rather than to the natural approach of the leader. So much for the theory, but of course most people are much more interested in how to put it into practice, which is where the skills of the trained facilitator are so valuable; in fact it is hard to see how anyone could do it without understanding the facilitator role and using the tools that underpin it. The effective use of Situational Leadership involves facilitative management, working with people, starting from where they are, with a view to the development of their levels of ability and willingness in the particular job such that, ultimately, they will be able, for the most part, to manage themselves. Reaching this point should be the real goal of every manager since it means that time and human resource are being used to best effect.

An increasing number of organizations encourage their high performers to spend time as practising facilitators. In some it has been made a formal part of the management development process for their up and coming people. The logic of this is that facilitators do not have organizational power in the conventional sense, and so they have to rely on using higher level skills if they are to be successful. Providing such people with the opportunity to work with others and to help them develop and improve their performance in the context of an organization improvement process, such as Organisation Development or Total Quality, is commonly found to be a very powerful way of improving their own individual performance when they return to their line management roles. Experience indicates that they show more sensitivity and skill in working with their people given this exposure, and that they are able to improve the performance of their departments, often substantially, by the continued application of the skills they have practised as facilitators.

There seems little doubt that effective management in the future will require an approach that meets the individual requirements of those being managed. Maybe it has always been so, but in the modern era people are much less willing to be treated *en masse*; they have higher expectations and are probably more aware of, and sensitive to, their 'rights' as individual and unique human beings.

It is because of these factors that facilitative management styles hold the key to good practice in the future, and there is enough evidence of the effectiveness of this way of doing things to suggest that organizations should begin to build the subject of facilitation and facilitator skills into the core agenda of their management development process. Further than this they should find ways of giving their managers the opportunity to practise these skills, to receive feedback and to work on improving their ability to manage in this way to the point that it is simply the normal way that things are done. The potential benefits of managing people more effectively are very significant, and in an increasingly competitive world we cannot afford to let an opportunity of this magnitude escape us.

As it stands today the role of the facilitator is largely performed separately from line management, and perhaps the biggest challenge that we face is that of integrating the principles and practice of this approach into the mainstream of the management process. When we achieve this we achieve our best chance of developing organizations that really do make the most of the immense latent talent that exists within them. It will be a long road, but one that the ultimate survivors and winners will travel with hope, enthusiasm and an unshakeable expectation of success.

Appendix
Situational leadership

Over the past few decades managers and management thinkers have been involved in a search for the 'best' style of leadership. Much useful work has been done, but the clearest result is that there appears to be no single all-purpose style that is universally ideal. Different ways of managing and leading appear to be more or less successful depending on the particular situation. For the practising facilitator a good working knowledge of this subject is essential, first because we are involved in the business of helping managers to become more effective, and second because in the course of our work we are actually 'managing' people, albeit without the executive authority usually associated with the managerial role.

Most people agree that the basic criteria in considering leadership style are:

- Task issues which are actions that concentrate attention on the particular task at hand in terms of what needs doing, when, where and how.
- Relationship issues which are actions that concentrate on the

feelings of the people doing the work and which provide support, help, understanding and explanation.

These two dimensions have been labelled in various ways by different people. For example task behaviour has been called 'autocratic', 'production centred', and 'concern for task', while relationship behaviour has been proposed as 'democratic', 'employee centred', and 'people oriented'.

Building on these concepts Hersey and Blanchard have developed their Situational Leadership model which concentrates attention on leader behaviour rather than concerns, predispositions and feelings. Situational Leadership Theory is based on interplay among:

- the amount of direction a leader gives
- the amount of support a leader gives
- the level of 'development' of the follower(s) in terms of the specific task at hand.

Directive behaviour is defined as: 'The extent to which a leader engages in one-way communication; spells out the follower(s) role and tells the follower(s) what to do, where to do it, when to do it and how to do it; and then closely supervises performance.' Three words can be used to define directive behaviour: structure, control and supervise.

Supportive behaviour is defined as: 'The extent to which a leader engages in two-way communications, listens, provides support and encouragement, facilitates interaction and involves the follower(s) in decision-making.' Three words can be used to define supportive behaviour: praise, listen and facilitate.

The concept of development level is central to Situational Leadership Theory. It is defined as the capacity to set high but attainable goals, willingness and ability to take responsibility, and the education/experience of the individual or group. These variables should only be considered in relation to the specific tasks at hand. The individual/group is not developed or underdeveloped in any total sense. For example, a sales representative might be very competent in the way he or she approaches his or her clients but not very developed at all in the writing of pro-

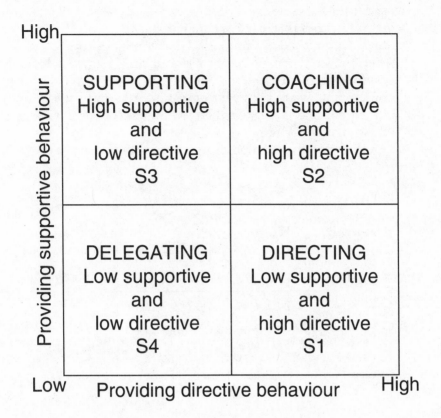

Figure A.1   Four basic leader behaviour styles
(Adapted from SLII – *A Situational Approach to Managing People*
by Ken Blanchard , 1985)

posals. The appropriate management style for these two situations will be different, reflecting the different levels of development.

Hersey and Blanchard's research identified four basic leader behaviour styles. The styles are very different and are shown in Figure A1.

According to Situational Leadership Theory, as the level of development of the follower increases in terms of accomplishing a specific task, the leader should begin to reduce directive behaviour and increase supportive behaviour. This should be the case until the individual or group reaches a moderate level of development, when it becomes appropriate for the leader to decrease not only directive behaviour but supportive behaviour as well. Now the follower is not only competent in terms of the performance of the task but also in their willingness to accept responsibility for it at this point.

Since the follower can provide his or her own reinforcement, a

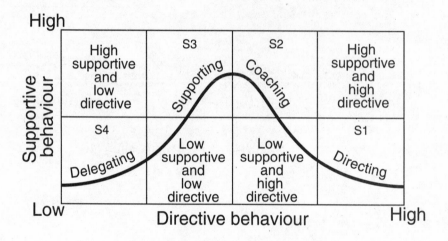

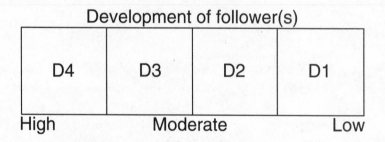

Figure A.2   Style of leader and development of follower
(Adapted from SLII – *A Situational Approach to Managing People*
by Ken Blanchard, 1985)

great deal of socio-emotional support from the leader is no longer necessary. People at this level see a reduction of close supervision and an increase in delegation by the leader as a positive indication of trust and confidence. Thus, Situational Leadership Theory concentrates on the appropriateness or effectiveness of leadership styles according to the development level of the follower(s). This cycle can be illustrated by a bell-shaped curve superimposed upon the four leadership quadrants, as illustrated in Figure A.2.

This figure shows the relationship between task-relevant competence and the appropriate leadership styles to be used as the follower moves from immaturity to maturity. It is important to keep in mind that the figure represents two different phenomena. The appropriate leadership style for given levels of follower competency is portrayed by the bell-shaped curve in the four leadership quadrants. The development level of the individual or group being supervised is shown below the leadership model as a continuum ranging from low to high competency.

The four basic leadership styles are referred to as:

- S1   high directive/low supportive
- S2   high directive/high supportive
- S3   low directive/high supportive
- S4   low directive/low supportive.

Four benchmarks of follower maturity are referred to as:

- D1   low levels of task-relevant competency
- D2   low to moderate levels of task-relevant competency
- D3   moderate to high levels of task-relevant competency
- D4   high levels of task-relevant competency.

To determine what leadership style is appropriate to use in a situation, one must first determine the development level of the follower in relation to the specific task that the leader is attempting to accomplish through the follower's efforts. Once this level is identified, the appropriate leadership style can be determined by constructing a right angle from the point where it intersects on the bell-shaped curve in the style of leader portion of the model. The quadrant in which that intersection takes place suggests the appropriate style to be used by the leader in that situation with a follower of the competency level.

Situational Leadership Theory contends that in working with people who are low in competency (D1) in terms of accomplishing a specific task, a high directive/low supportive style (S1) has the highest probability of success: in dealing with people who are of low to moderate competency (D2), a high directive/high supportive style (S2) appears to be most appropriate: in working with people who are of moderate to high competency (D3) in terms of accomplishing a specific task, a high supportive/low directive (S3) has the highest probability of success: in working with people of high task-relevant competency (D4) a low directive/low supportive (S4) style has the highest probability of success.

While it is important to keep in mind the definitions of directive and supportive behaviour given earlier, the labelling of the four styles of Situational Leadership Theory, as follows, is sometimes useful for quick diagnostic judgements:

- *High directive/low supportive leader behaviour* (S1) is referred to as 'directing' because this style is characterized by one-way communication in which the leader defines the roles of followers and tells them what, how, when and where to do various tasks.
- *High directive/high supportive behaviour* (S2) is referred to as 'coaching' because with this style most of the direction is still provided by the leader. He or she also attempts through two-way communication and socio-emotional support to get the followers psychologically to buy into decisions that have to be made.
- *High supportive/low directive behaviour* (S3) is called 'supporting' because with this style the leader and follower(s) now share in decision-making through two-way communication and much facilitating behaviour from the leaders since the follower(s) have the ability and knowledge to do the task.
- *Low supportive/low directive behaviour* (S4) is called 'delegat-

ing' because with this style the leader hands over responsibility to the follower. As the follower is not only competent in a task sense but also psychologically independent, little relationship behaviour is required.

The implication of the theory is that the manager progressively develops the maturity of his or her follower(s) and changes his or her style accordingly.

In attempting to develop the followers who have not taken much responsibility in the past, a leader must be careful not to increase supportive behaviour too rapidly. If this is done, the followers may view the leader as becoming a 'soft touch'. Thus the leader must develop followers slowly using a little less directive behaviour and a little more supportive behaviour as followers mature. When an individual's performance is low, one cannot expect drastic changes overnight.

For more desirable behaviour to be obtained, a leader must reward as quickly as possible the slightest appropriate behaviour exhibited by the individual in the desired direction and continue this process as the individual's behaviour comes closer and closer to the leader's expectations of good performance. For example, if a leader wants to improve the development level of a follower so this follower will assume significantly more responsibility, the leader's best option initially is to reduce a little of the direction by giving the follower an opportunity to assume some increased responsibility. If this responsibility is well-handled, the leader should reinforce this behaviour with increases in supportive behaviour. This is a two-step process: first, reduction in direction, and if adequate performance follows, second, increase in supportive behaviour as reinforcement.

This process should continue until the follower is assuming significant responsibility and performing as an individual of moderate development level. This does not mean that the individual's work will have less direction, but the direction will now be internally imposed by the follower rather than externally imposed by the leader. As this process occurs, followers are not only able to complete the task with little direction, they provide their own satisfaction for interpersonal and emotional needs. At

this stage, followers are positively reinforced for accomplish-
ments not by the leader looking over their shoulder but by the
leader leaving them more and more on their own. It is not that
there is less mutual trust and friendship (in fact, there is more)
but it takes less direct effort on the leader's part to prove it with
more independent followers.

Although this theory seems to suggest a basic style for different levels of competence it is not quite that simple. When followers begin to behave less skillfully, for whatever reason, for
example a crisis at home or a change in work technology, it
becomes appropriate and necessary for leaders to adjust their
behaviour backwards through the bell-shaped curve to meet the
maturity level of the followers. For example, a subordinate who
is presently working well without much supervision who suddenly encounters a family crisis which begins to affect his or her
performance on the job will need managing with more direction
and support until he or she regains composure.

Take another example of a teacher who was highly motivated
and competent (D4) and therefore could be left alone. Suppose
he or she is promoted to headteacher. While it may have been
appropriate to leave well alone and delegate (S4) as a teacher,
now in a different role and with little experience, it may be
appropriate for the supervisor to change styles by first providing
more socio-emotional support and then increasing the amount
of direction and supervision of activities (S4 to S3 to S2). This
high directive/high supportive style should continue until the
person is able to grasp the new responsibilities. At that time a
movement back from S2 through S3 to S4 would be appropriate.
Starting off using the same leadership style that was successful
while the person concerned was a teacher, may now prove ineffective because it is inappropriate for the new situation.

In summary, effective leaders must know their staff well and
be able to manage their different levels of ability and willingness
by using different styles. It should be remembered that, over
time, followers as individuals and as groups develop their own
patterns of behaviour and ways of operating. While a leader may
use a specific style for the work group as a group, that leader
may quite often have to behave differently with individual fol-

lowers because they are at different levels of competency. In either case, whether working with a group or an individual, changes in leadership from S1 to S2, S3 and S4, must be gradual! This process by its very nature cannot be revolutionary but must be evolutionary.

Leaders therefore need to:

- be flexible in style
- diagnose accurately the appropriate style to employ
- negotiate effectively with followers about the style to be used.

Sources and resources

Organization change and development

Books

The Journey to Excellence by Mike Robson (MRA International, 1986).
This contains a coherent model for the development of organizations and the achievement of sustained excellence. It incorporates the principles and practice of Total Quality.

Organisation Development by Warner Burke (Addison Wesley, 1987).
This provides an overview of the field of Organisation Development (OD), and includes a definition, the models of change that OD has been based on historically, and chapters on the process and management of change.

Process Consultation (vols 1 and 2) by Edgar Schein (Addison Wesley, 1987 and 1988).

These books describe 'process consultation' and the alternative styles of consultancy. They include much useful advice for the internal or external consultant who wishes to learn about and develop a capability in process consultancy.

Other resources
The Journey to Excellence – the Mike Robson Approach to Quality (BBC video pack, 1987).
This is a double video pack which contains an explanation of this powerful model of change, and case histories from four organizations that have used it, complete with user guide.

Groups and group problem-solving

Books
Management Teams, Why They Succeed or Fail by R. Meredith Belbin (Heinemann, 1981).
This is Belbin's main book on the subject of team roles. It includes a detailed explanation of the different roles, and material describing unsuccessful and successful teams. It also contains a self-perception inventory.

Decision Making in Small Groups by Albert Kowitz and Thomas Knutson (Allyn and Bacon, 1980).
This is a technical book which includes sections on the structure of interactions, groups and decisions. It also analyses group process problems. It is useful if you are interested in studying groups, but is not easy to read.

Group Dynamics by Marvin Shaw (McGraw Hill, 1971).
This is a technical book which is not easy to read, but it deals with some of the basics of group dynamics, for example group size, seating and other special arrangements, the social structure of groups, the task environment and different types of group.

Problem Solving in Groups by Mike Robson (Gower, 1993).
This book is a practical guide to solving problems in groups. It

contains a step-by-step problem-solving process, and includes the detail of how to use the different techniques successfully. Some of the techniques that are included are well-known, others are new.

Quality Circles – A Practical Guide (2nd Edition) by Mike Robson (Gower, 1992).
This is a comprehensive guide to the theory and practice of one of the key concepts that transformed Japan. It contains a detailed account of how to introduce and sustain the approach. Though often given a different name today, the approach is widely used by successful organizations.

Other resources
Problem Solving in Groups by Mike Robson (Connaught Training video pack, 1993).
This is a double video pack: the first deals with issues of group process and the second on the problem-solving structure, including how to use many of the techniques. It contains imaginative use of archive footage. Includes user guide with visual aids.

Quality First by Mike Robson (Connaught Training video pack, 1993).
This video provides work groups with a coherent process that will enable them to improve their performance in agreeing and then meeting the requirements of their internal and external customers. Includes user guide and additional visual aids.

Individual behaviour

Books
I'm OK – You're OK by Thomas Harris (Pan, 1970).
This is the seminal work on life positions. The book contains material on transactional analysis, which was the basis of Harris's ideas on life positions, and so it is useful in that it covers both subjects in sufficient depth. It is also easy to read and digest.

Motivation and Personality by Abraham Maslow (Harper and Row, 1970).
This was one of Maslow's main books. It is not particularly easy to read, but it contains interesting and useful material on his hierarchy of needs model, and goes into a lot of detail on the much misunderstood idea of self-actualization.

Understanding People by Boshear and Albrecht (University Associates, 1977).
This is a practical book that acts as a toolkit for people who are involved with the development of others. It contains material about individuals, pairs, groups, organizations, and a range of supplementary concepts.

On Becoming a Person by Carl Rogers (Houghton Mifflin, 1993).
This book describes the principles and the practicalities of client-centred therapy. It contains a significant amount of case material. It is not a very easy book, but it deals with a concept that is important in understanding the facilitator role.

Neuro-Linguistic Programming (NLP)

Books
Frogs into Princes by Richard Bandler and John Grinder (Real People Press, 1976).
This book contains the transcript from a seminar run by the two authors who were the founders of NLP. It covers some of the basic concepts and is a good introduction to the subject.

The Structure of Magic (vols 1 and 2) by John Grinder and Richard Bandler (SBB, 1976)
These books go into greater detail about the subject of NLP. It probably makes sense to read *Frogs into Princes* first and then to begin a more serious study with these two books.

Using Your Brain – For a Change by Richard Bandler (Real People Press, 1985).
This is a more recent book by Richard Bandler and is an edited compilation of a number of his seminars. In it he introduces some of the newer techniques and patterns that he has found to be useful, including ways of changing beliefs, curing phobias and turning bad experiences into positive ones.

Index

209